THE CLASSICAL GUITAR TECHNIQUE BOOK

The Complete Guide To Mastering Modern Classical Guitar Technique

DIEGO **PRATO**

FUNDAMENTAL CHANGES

The Classical Guitar Technique Book

The Complete Guide To Mastering Modern Classical Guitar Technique

ISBN: 978-1-78933-124-0

Published by www.fundamental-changes.com

Copyright © 2019 Diego Prato

Edited by Tim Pettingale

The moral right of this author has been asserted.

All rights reserved. No part of this publication may be reproduced, stored in a retrieval system, or transmitted in any form or by any means, without the prior permission in writing from the publisher.

The publisher is not responsible for websites (or their content) that are not owned by the publisher.

www.fundamental-changes.com

Twitter: @guitar_joseph

Over 10,000 fans on Facebook: **FundamentalChangesInGuitar**

Instagram: **FundamentalChanges**

For over 350 Free Guitar Lessons with Videos Check Out

www.fundamental-changes.com

Cover Image Copyright: Shutterstock, Alenavlad

Contents

Things to Keep in Mind While Working Through This Book — 4

Holding the Guitar and Positioning the Hands — 6

Chapter One: Fretting Hand Finger Control and Independence — 9

Chapter Two: Position Shifting — 21

Chapter Three: Legato — 27

Chapter Four: Developing and Refining Tone with the Picking Hand — 39

Chapter Five: Arpeggio Playing — 50

Chapter Six: Rapid Arpeggio Patterns — 60

Chapter Seven: Training the Thumb — 66

Chapter Eight: Finger-Thumb Alternation and Tremolo — 73

Chapter Nine: Refining Scales and Single-Line Melodic Playing — 78

Chapter Ten: Fretboard-Long Repositioned Scale Shapes — 88

Chapter Eleven: Speed and Dexterity for Rest Strokes — 91

Chapter Twelve: Rasgueado — 100

Chapter Thirteen: Controlling Your Breathing — 106

Final Thoughts — 108

More Classical Guitar Books From Fundamental Changes — 109

Things to Keep in Mind While Working Through This Book

Musicality

This book has been designed to help you push your technical ability on the classical guitar as far as possible. However, any good classical guitarist knows that the ultimate goal of any exercise is to help you produce the most beautiful sound possible. Some technical exercises don't sound very musical, but you should always aim for a beautiful tone and constantly use your ears to refine the sound coming from your instrument. It doesn't matter whether you're playing a single, repeating note as a warm-up routine, or a masterpiece by a celebrated composer – keep the integrity of your tone. Many players ignore musicality when working on technique, so don't waste the opportunity to improve and refine your tone while working on your technique!

Read the text and follow the method

I've taught the guitar for many years and seen lots of students work their way through various books. My observation is that players will often approach their studies in a very disorganised way. They skip chapters, skip exercises, and often don't read the guidance that accompanies each exercise or area of study.

All good method books are carefully planned and designed in a logical order, so that everything is there for a reason. Each exercise gives the ideal preparation for the next one. The text is there to make you aware of key details to concentrate on as you work on the exercise. Without these details, the exercise can lose its benefit.

So, when working through this book please ensure that you *always*:

- Master each exercise before moving on to the next
- Do every exercise and don't skip any exercises/chapters
- Read the text carefully to ensure you're playing the exercises correctly and making the most of the book

Exercise repetition

Play the exercises in this book for a number of weeks, even after you can already play them well. This will ensure that the response of your fingers has improved as much as possible. The goal is not to finish the book as soon as you can, but to really internalise all the techniques.

Tempos

The most important thing is to play these exercises well. Playing them fast does *not* mean you have cultivated great technique, it just means you can play them badly faster! The exercises in this book have been carefully designed to get your muscles working in ways they are not used to, so that the work will be harder and the results produced will be better. It's therefore much more important to play them perfectly at slower tempos and only gradually increase the speed.

Push yourself, but don't injure yourself

If you are committed to improving as a player, then you are bound to push yourself to do better and repeat demanding exercises. This is important for your technical development, but don't put undue stress on your hands and fingers. Just as you wouldn't try to immediately pick up a massive weight in the gym, you need to gradually increase your capacity. Take plenty of rests and over time you'll find you can demand more of your muscles. Your hands and fingers might feel tired after a lot of playing, which is fine, but if it hurts, stop!

Holding the Guitar and Positioning the Hands

Traditional Classical Posture

The images above show the traditional posture for classical guitar. Notice the slightly tilted angle of the instrument, which causes the sound hole to face upwards. This posture achieves two goals:

- It allows the player to have the best access to the instrument
- It ensures the guitar projects its sound as efficiently as possible

As an experiment, position your guitar with the lower curve resting fully on your right leg and without using a footstool. Try playing something. Now move to traditional posture. Hopefully you can see that the non-classical approach means having to stretch considerably further to fret the strings. It also means having to hunch over to see the frets. With the correct posture you can keep a straight back and still easily see the frets.

The tilted position of the guitar in classical posture results in improved tone production and projection. The sound travels upwards, filling the space where you are playing, rather than projecting straight out/downwards. This position also allows the back of the guitar to resonate more freely, producing more sound, rather than being damped by the player's stomach.

Modern approaches to classical posture

In the modern era, players have found alternative ways of keeping the benefits of classical posture while avoiding the fatigue that can be placed on the lower back due to the raised leg on the footstool. An alternative is to use an A-frame or other device on their thigh, which raises the guitar without having to raise the leg. See the image below.

Thumb positioning

When playing, ensure your left- and right-hand thumbs are always straight. The picking thumb should only move from where it joins your hand, never from its secondary joint. This will give it greater mobility and reduce fatigue. The fretting hand thumb should never bend and must never press with exaggerated force. Its job is to provide only the necessary support for the fingers at the front.

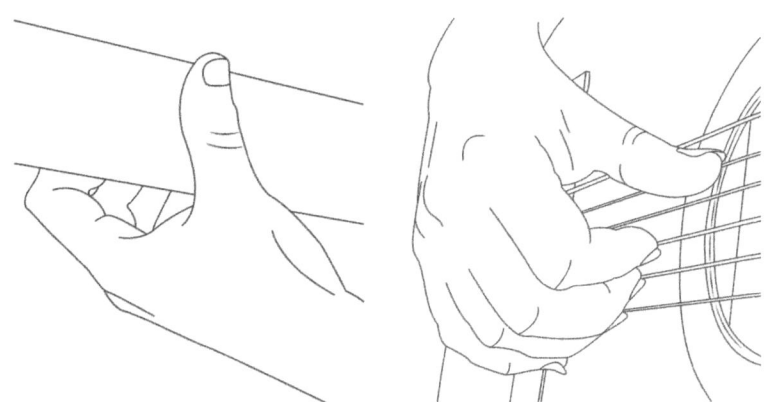

Wrist positioning

How the wrists function when playing is a critical factor in enabling the hands to play as efficiently as possible. Like the thumbs, both left- and right-hand wrists should always be straight. This may be difficult to achieve at first. Rather than bending the wrists, the angle of the arm and curvature of the fingers should play the main role in allowing your hand to reach the frets comfortably. Work gradually and patiently on this. It may take longer than expected, but it is critical for long-term technical success. The idea is to avoid any unnecessary tension to our muscles, tendons and bones. Free, unobstructed, movement must be pursued at all times.

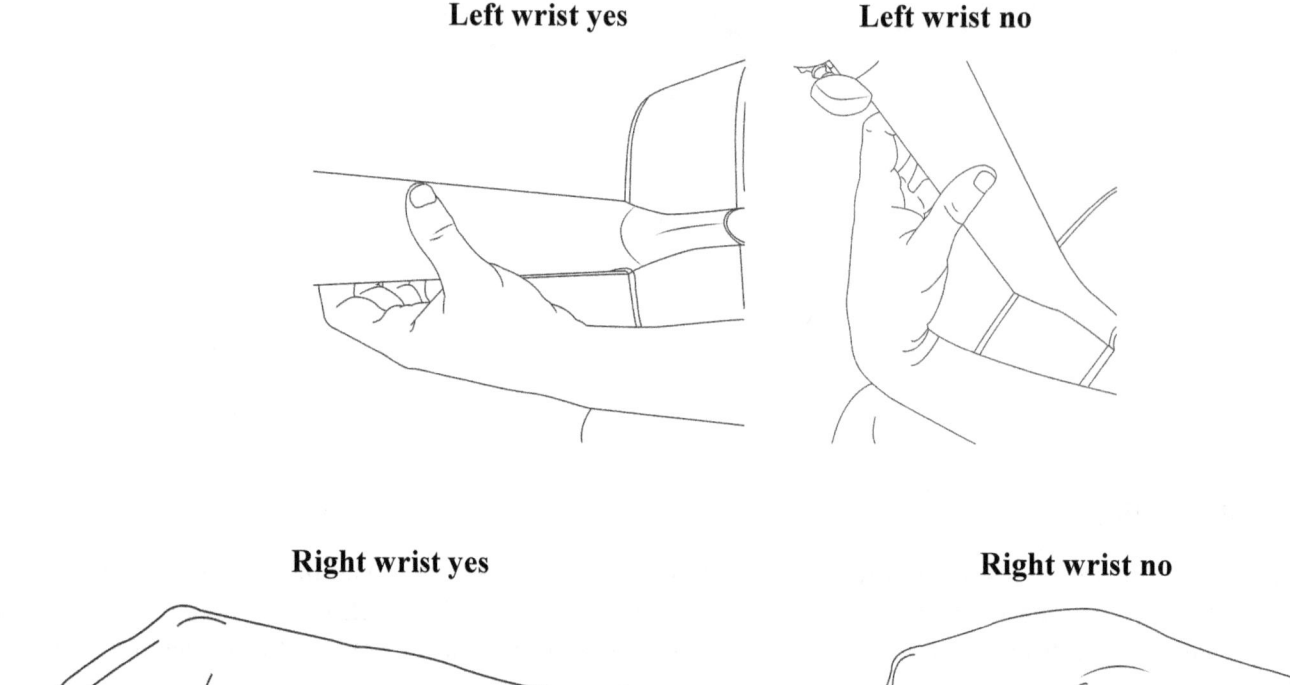

General body management

It may not be obvious at times, but all the main parts of our body are engaged when we play guitar. The way we sit, the way we breathe, the tension in our shoulders all have a considerable effect on the sound we are able to produce from our instrument. Just like our hands/wrists, we need to avoid any unnecessary tension and be relaxed.

When you play, make a habit of monitoring your body as well as your hands. Keep an eye on your shoulders. Are they high up? They should be relaxed. Are you tensing any muscles? If so, concentrate on relaxing them for a few seconds. Are you putting all the weight of your leg through your toes? Ensure that you rest your foot flat on the floor or foot stool!

Chapter One: Fretting Hand Finger Control and Independence

Keeping the fingers close to the strings

For classical guitarists, economy of movement and the efficient use of energy is critical. Without these factors in place, the technical challenges of the style can get in the way of the ultimate goal: beautiful, unobstructed music making.

When playing, the good management of those fingers which are not in use is as important as those that are. By keeping the fingers close to the strings, we are in the best position to play each next note as effectively and musically as possible. Additionally, we reduce fatigue.

The following exercises are carefully designed to help you train your fingers to stay close to the strings at all times. Each should be repeated three to four times at the beginning of every practice session and should become a part of your long-term warm-up routine.

These workouts must be done *very* slowly at first, played free time, not to a tempo. The only thing you need to pay attention to is that the fingers do the right work.

In Example 1a, press down the first four notes *simultaneously* on the 6th string, using the fingers as indicated. Then play the passage that follows keeping each finger pressed down on its original note until it needs to play a new one. As each finger reaches a new note, again hold the note down continuously until it needs to move. So, each finger will go from continuously holding down one note to continuously holding down another, without rest, until the end of the exercise.

Make sure that your fretting hand thumb is kept behind the neck, with its joint straight. It can move slightly up or down depending on the demands of the passage but should never be raised above the neck to any significant extent.

Example 1a

Now continue with the next two exercises following the same principle. Hold down the notes *continuously*. Once a finger plays a note, it must continue to hold it down until it must move to a new one, as before.

Example 1b

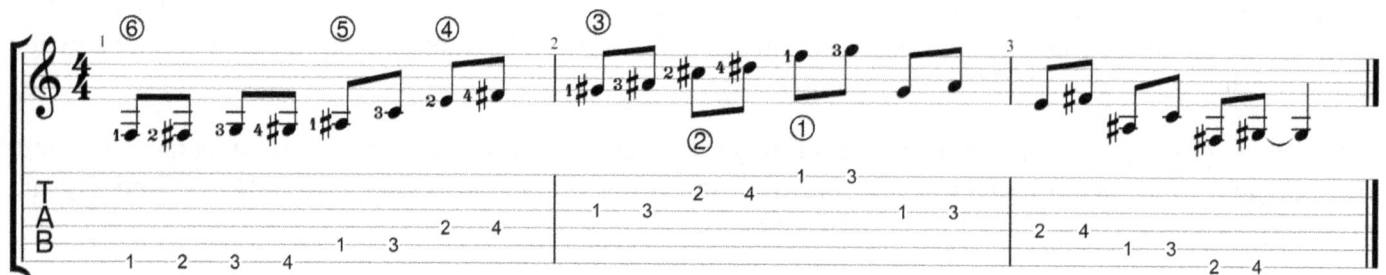

The next exercise requires more stretching from the fretting hand. If you find that any of your fingers struggle to reach the notes on the 6th (low E) string, simply play up to the note on the same fret on the 5th (A) string. This stretch should be easier, while not affecting the benefit of the exercise.

Example 1c

Rested fingers exercises

The following exercises are the next step towards excellent finger management and positioning. They will train your non-playing fingers to move from applying constant pressure to only *resting* on the strings. These exercises are equally challenging, however, because they still require a high degree of control. It can be more difficult to continuously touch the strings *without* pressing them, while other fingers move around.

Exercise 1d will train the independence of each finger individually. Be patient, move *very* slowly and forget about any sense of tempo. Take as much time as you need to control your fingers enough to do it.

For this exercise, only *rest* your fingers on the first four notes. Don't press down and don't lift them. Keep all non-playing fingers in this exact position at all times throughout the exercise. Be very strict with yourself as this is the main challenge of the exercise as well as its real benefit.

If you haven't done this kind of exercise before, you will notice how much concentration it takes to keep the fingers resting. Remember, ignore tempo! This is not like other guitar exercises where being able to play fast is an indication of your progress. The slower you do this exercise, the more your fingers will benefit, especially in the early stages.

Example 1d

The next exercise is a natural progression from Example 1d. It takes the fingers from moving between strings two (B) and five (A), to moving between strings one (high E) and six (low E).

Example 1e

Now you will start to increase the movement between different fingers, getting close to the idea of moving fingers in opposite directions simultaneously (which you will do more of in a moment). Make sure that you continue to only *rest,* not press, your non-playing fingers on the first four notes.

Example 1f

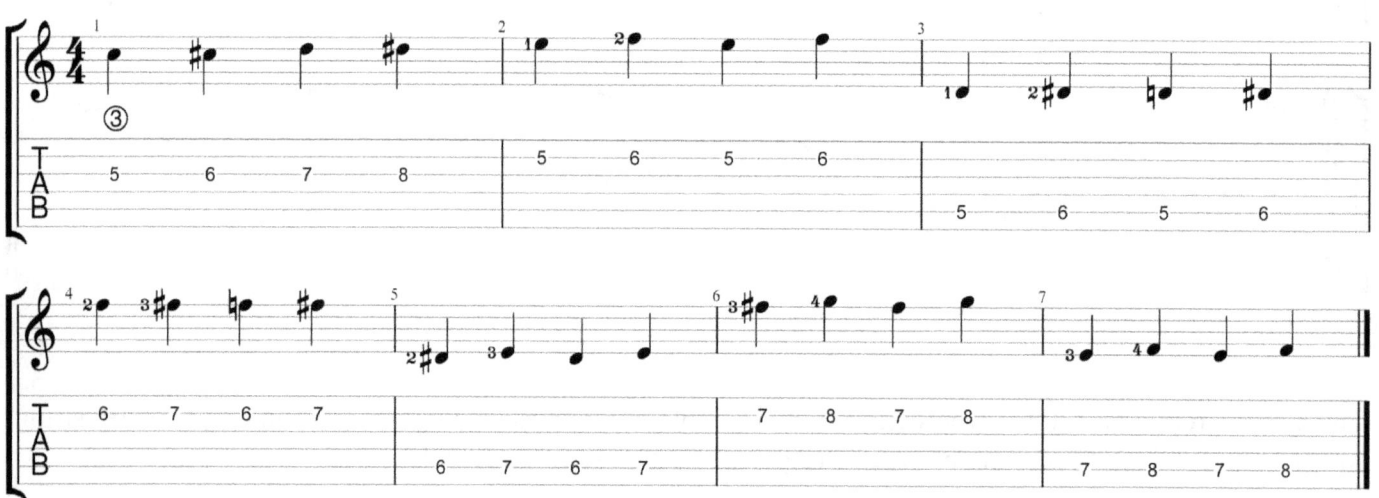

Let's take the previous exercise a step further by taking the fingers from working between strings two (B) and five (A), to moving between strings one (high E) and six (low E).

Example 1g

Finger independence

The next challenge is to move two playing fingers in opposite directions simultaneously, while continuing to *rest* the remaining, non-playing fingers. Aim to move both fingers at the same time, rather than relocating each one separately. This way you will really be working on the skill of independence. Patience is key!

Keep reminding yourself, the first four notes are only to be *rested* on simultaneously. Keep all non-playing fingers focused on this throughout the exercise (don't lift, don't press!)

Example 1h

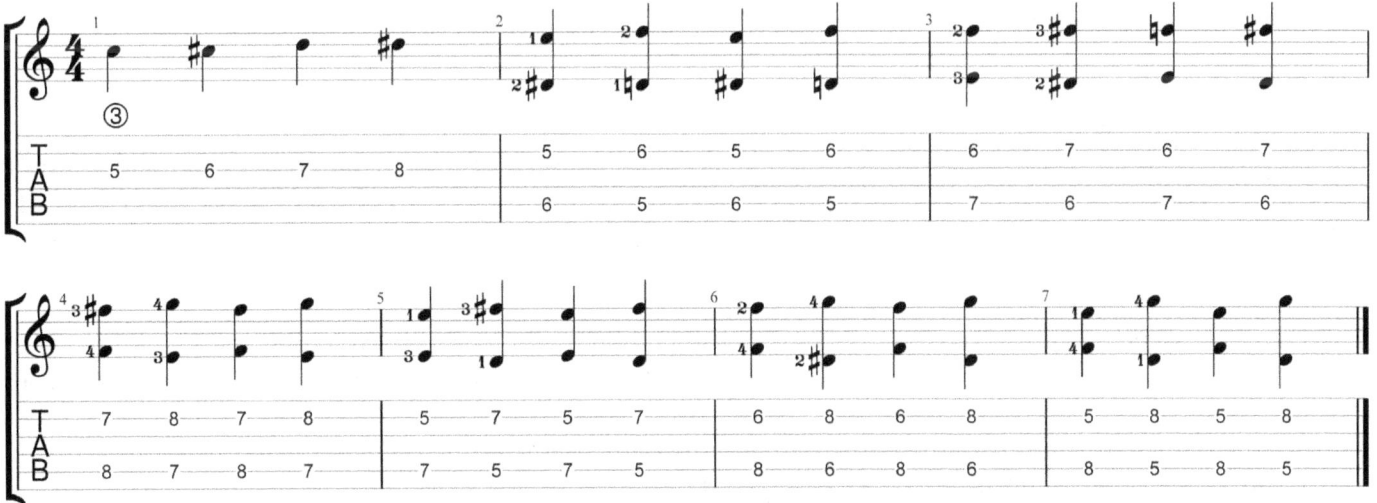

If we can master a stretch between strings two (B) and five (A), we must strive to take it to the next level: strings one (high E) and six (low E). However, be careful not to push your hand beyond the limits of what it should be doing at any given time or you may end up with an injury. If you are still working hard to play Example 1h, don't try this exercise yet – take a break!

Example 1i

Well done! You have completed all the rested finger exercises. Most players find that once they master these exercises, it gives their fingers a great deal of control. After many years, I still incorporate them into my regular practice routine and I suggest that you do the same as your playing develops!

Preparing fretting hand fingers

The purpose of the next section is to train the fretting hand fingers to move towards the next note in the music long before they need to play it. (As opposed to immediately before, as many players do). Of course, the opportunity to do this will be affected by the particular passage of music you are playing, and the note values in it, but developing this skill will greatly reduce the effort needed to play any passage – especially a demanding one. It also creates a smooth flow of phrases and preserves the quality of the sound, avoiding rushed or forced movements.

Following are some exercises based on octaves. These will help you focus on stretching and moving pairs of fingers simultaneously. Speed is not important; playing slower means your fingers get more out of the work they are doing.

Try to move your fingers towards each successive note (or pair of notes) as much in advance as you can. As soon as you have played a note, the finger responsible for playing the next one should be on the move.

As you work on the exercise below, strive to move each pair of fingers together and keep them as synchronised as you can. This exercise is very demanding, so if you feel your hand is being pushed too hard, stop! You can play a small number of bars to begin with, then gradually do more as your fingers get used to the work.

Example 1j

The next exercise is a variation of the previous one. It is also demanding and combines elements of finger independence and stretching. Make sure you hold each note for its full time value.

Example 1k

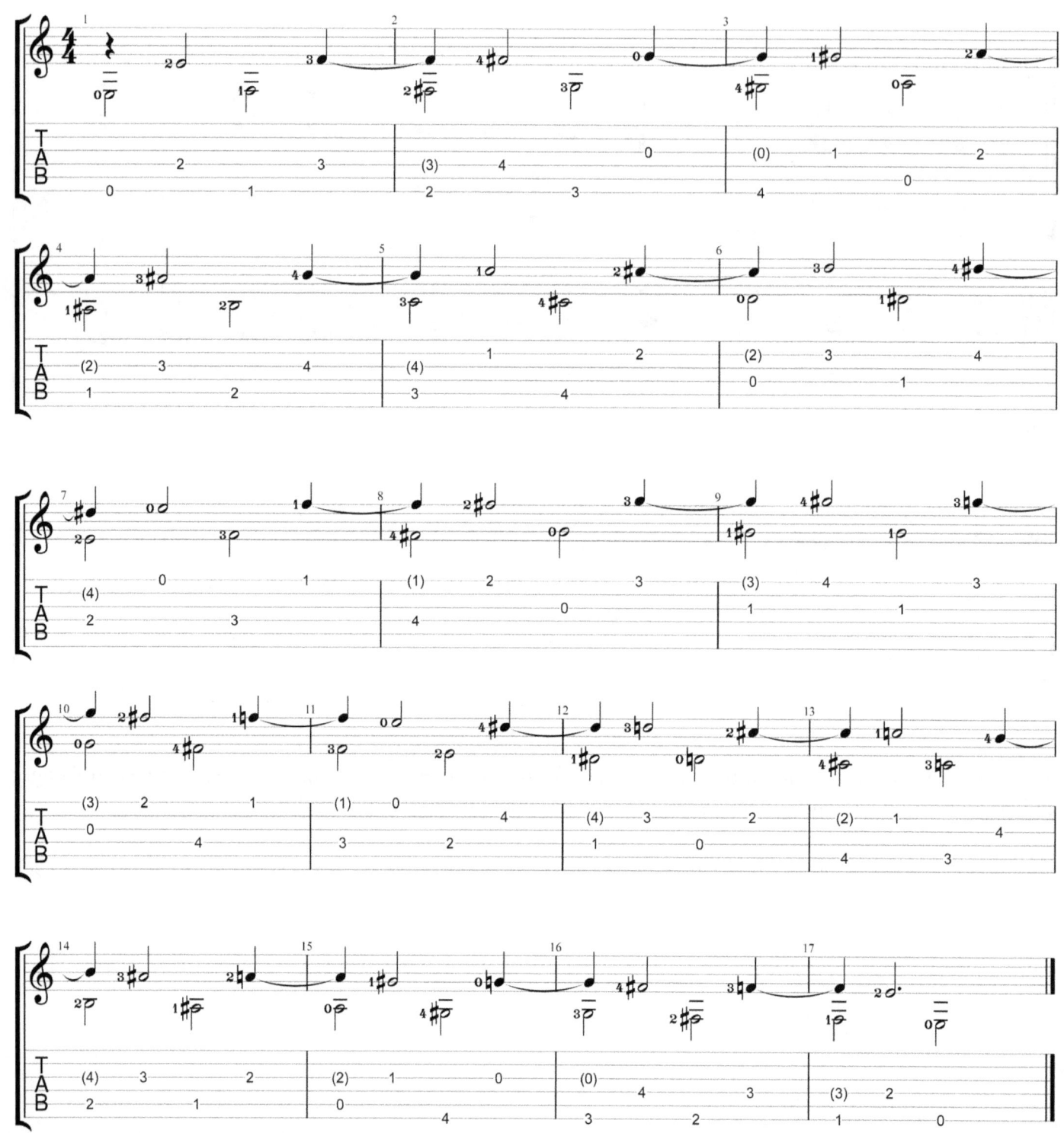

Monitoring your fingers during regular playing

So far, the workouts in this book have been carefully designed to help your fretting hand fingers behave in an efficient and highly responsive manner, considerably increasing the amount of control you have over them.

From this point on, your goal is to apply these principles to your normal playing. Go through your existing repertoire and play it slowly, keeping your fingers as close to the strings as possible. Move to each new note as far in advance as possible. For a while, while your fingers are being trained, you will have to *force* them to do what they are told! In the beginning, it may feel like you are moving your fingers down from their natural resting position in order to keep them close the strings. This is normal and part of the process of gaining a higher level of control over your fingers. After a while, this won't require so much effort and will become natural.

Pressing the correct amount

As you move towards a higher level of technique, one of the main goals is to reduce the amount of energy expended to the minimum required. In other words, developing the skill of using only the essential force needed to play a note and no more.

Our instinct is to press down on the strings harder than necessary. We know that pressing harder than we need to will still produce the right sound, whereas not pressing hard enough will produce a poor sound or a buzz. But pressing too hard requires more effort and makes it hard to move the fingers to fret each new note.

You can practice this by repeatedly playing any fretted note on your guitar. Start by just *resting* on it, then gradually add pressure until the note rings clearly. Once you can hear the clear sound of the note, notice how much force you had to apply. You may be surprised to learn that it didn't require very much force.

Below is a simple G Major scale. This is an exercise in applying just enough pressure to play the scale cleanly. Work on applying the *minimum force* to make each note ring clearly, and no more.

Example 11

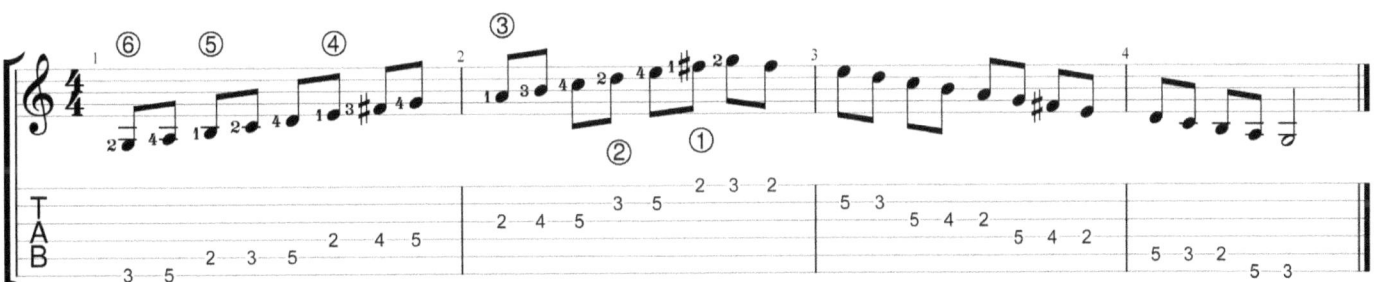

Applying all principles for the fretting hand

As you play the final exercise of this chapter, I want you to apply *all* the basic principles discussed so far.

- Keep your fingers close to the strings
- Prepare your fingers for each new note as far in advance as possible
- Only use the minimum required force to sound each note clearly
- Tempo is not important. The accurate and disciplined completion of the exercise is where the benefit lies

Exercise 1m

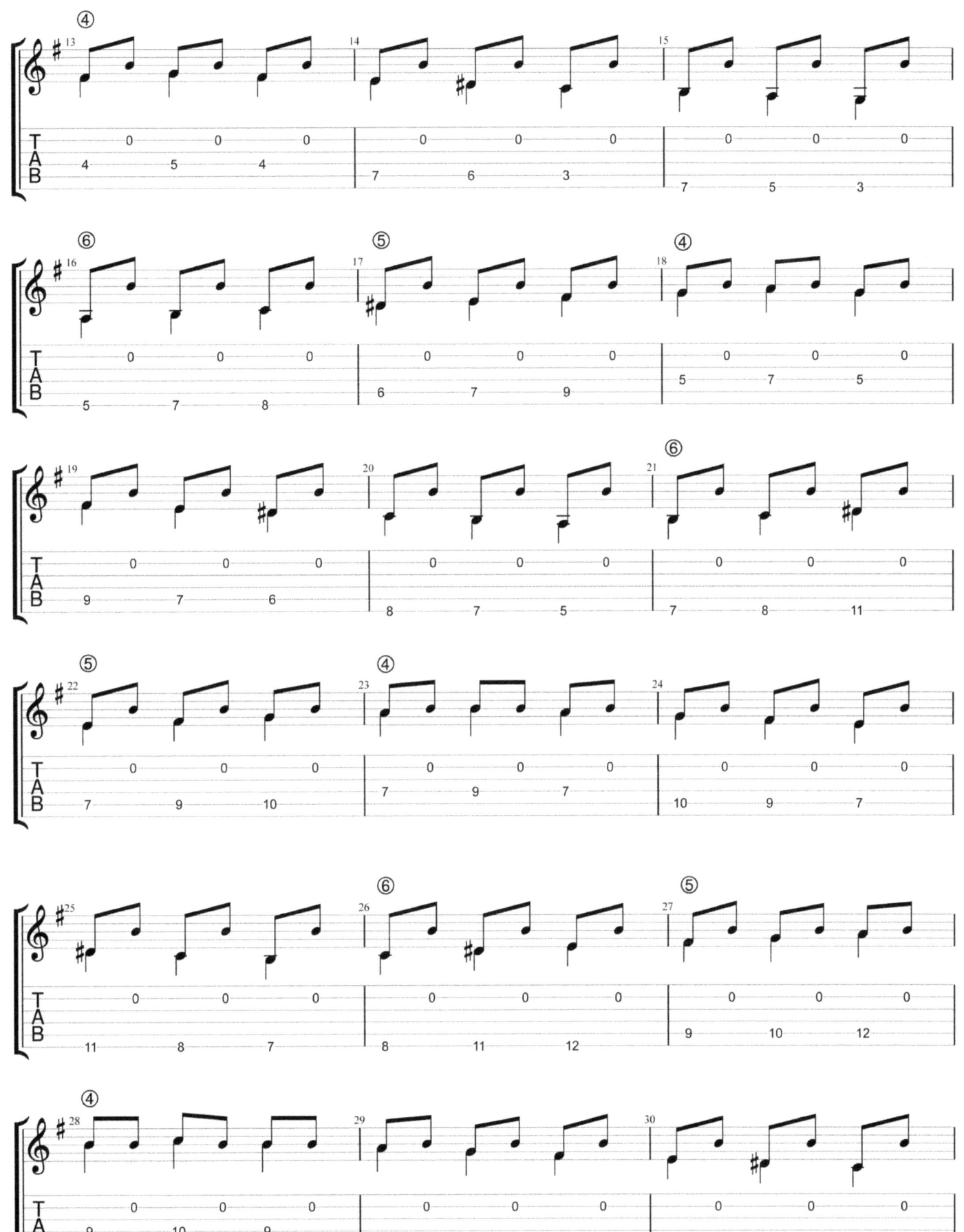

Chapter Two: Position Shifting

In this section you will work on an essential aspect of fretting hand classical guitar technique – one which is often overlooked by guitar teachers: the concept of position shifting during ascending and descending phrases.

Position shifting is an effective way to access notes that are higher (or lower) in register than those available in your current playing position. We might also move position to achieve a change in tone colour produced by a different area of the fretboard.

Position shifting requires logically planning how the fretting hand fingers will work as they move up and down a string, to prevent any unnecessary stretches, minimise the effort required, and produce a smooth musical result.

As a general rule, we aim to never stretch our fingers beyond the four-fret range of a given position, whether we are going up or down the fretboard. Instead, we shift the whole hand into a new position. Additionally, we aim to never use the same finger more than twice in succession. The only time we might need to deviate from these rules is when playing very high up the fretboard, where the distance between frets is much smaller.

The examples below feature the same musical phrase three times, played on the same string and frets. Examples 2a and 2b are played without applying the principles above. Examples 2b and 2c show alternative ways of using a position shift.

Example 2a

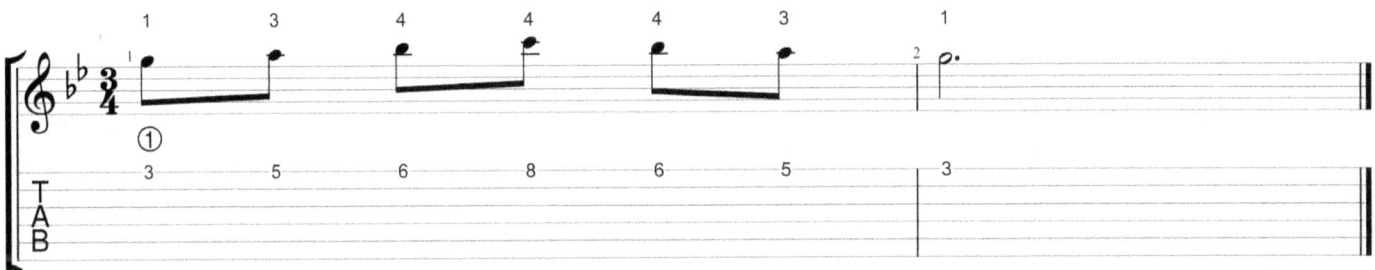

As you can see in the above example, the little finger has to do a lot more work than the other fingers. The workload is not spread evenly, and this makes it harder to produce a high-quality musical result.

Although the version in Example 2b allows us to stay pretty close to our original position, the whole hand is now having to stretch considerably, creating unnecessary strain. Again, it makes it harder to play an easy-flowing musical line.

Example 2b

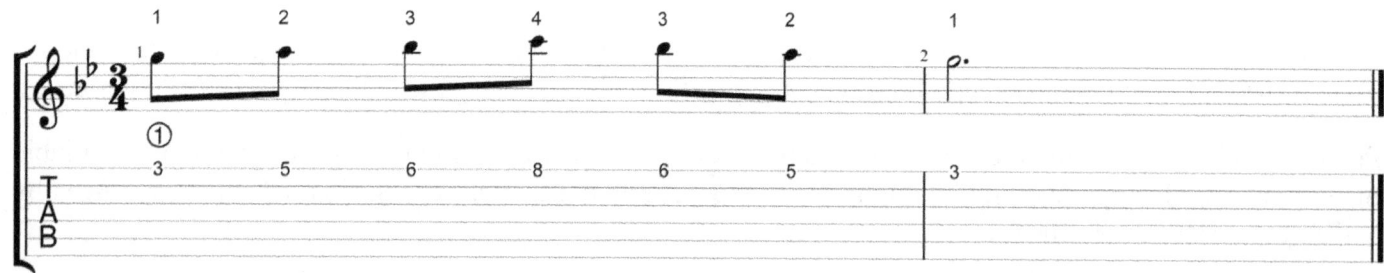

In the following version there is no stretching and there are no fingers playing more than two notes in a row. This balances the workload and avoids unnecessary stretches.

Example 2c

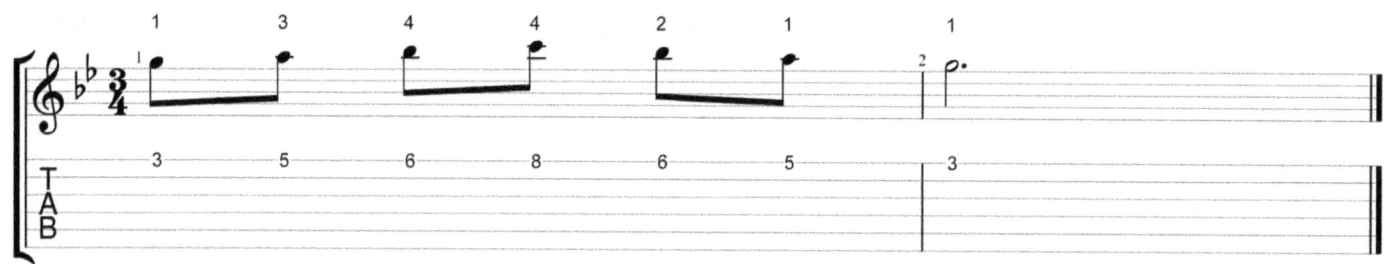

Below is an alternative option which would be appropriate as long as the phrase is not repeated two or more times in a row (otherwise the index finger would end up playing three consecutive times once the phrase starts to repeat).

Example 2d

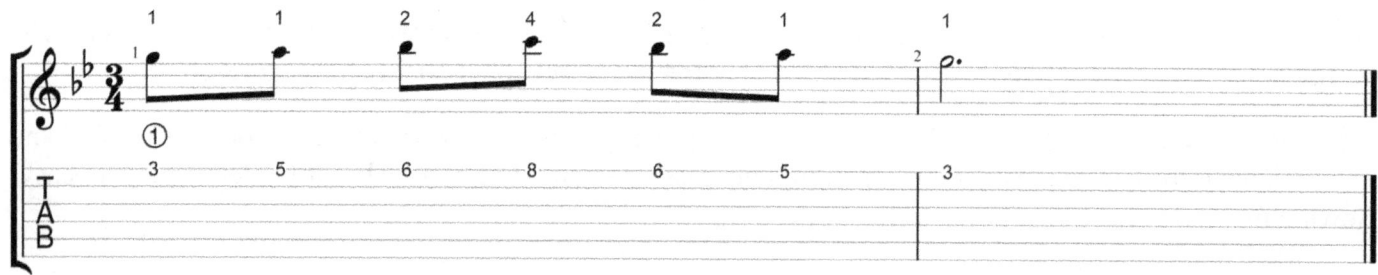

Arguably, the first two ways of playing the line above could be described as more instinctive. Prior to receiving formal training, many guitarists tend to play phrases in this way. The latter two are more complicated in terms of coordination, so require more thought. But once this hurdle is overcome, the movement will feel much easier. Gradually cultivate this approach to playing such phrases when you see them and it will be one of the best investments you make into your classical guitar technique. Fingering indications in repertoire will often demand this kind of approach, so work in this area will be time very well spent!

Now we will play a few different scales to get your fingers accustomed to using this technique. Be patient and concentrate on using the correct fingers as indicated. Transfer each scale pattern to all the other strings on the guitar. This will help with training and will provide you with the exact same scale types in new keys.

Play very slowly and repeat each exercise several times over a good few days in order to get the most out of them. You should use alternating *i* and *m* fingers on the picking hand for all these exercises, starting with either of them. This breaks away with tradition a little bit (lines on the D, A and low E strings are usually played with the thumb) but will help you build speed and concentrate on the task at hand.

Don't worry at this point about whether you are using free strokes or rest strokes. The fretting hand is the priority at this point. Other chapters will concentrate on the picking hand aspects of technique.

Example 2e F major scale (one string position shift exercise)

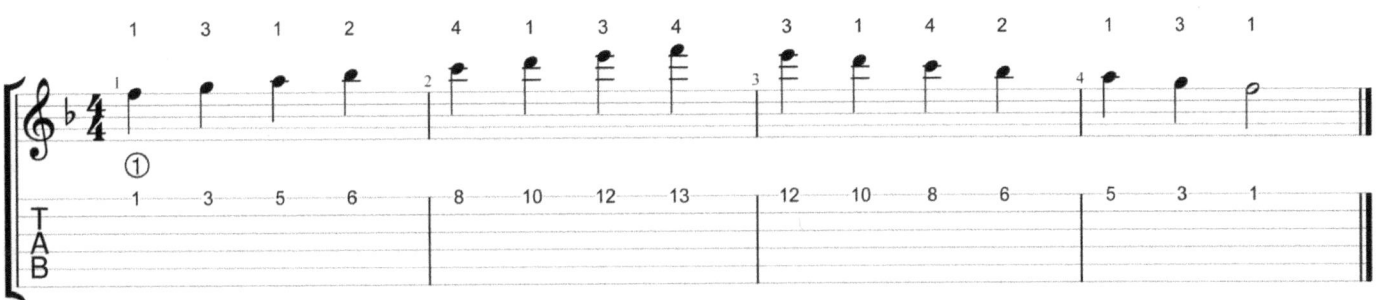

F natural minor scale (one string position shift exercise)

Example 2f

F Harmonic minor scale (one string position shift exercise)

Example 2g

F Melodic minor scale (one string position shift exercise)

Example 2h

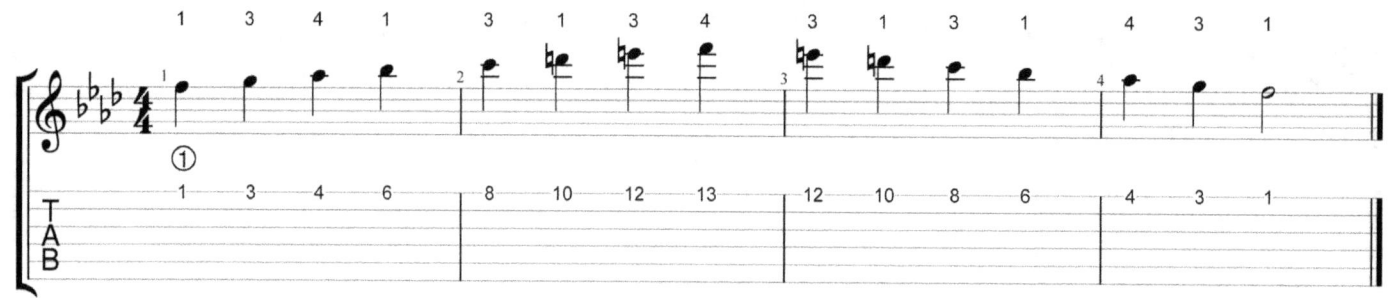

F chromatic scale (one string position shift exercise)

Example 2i

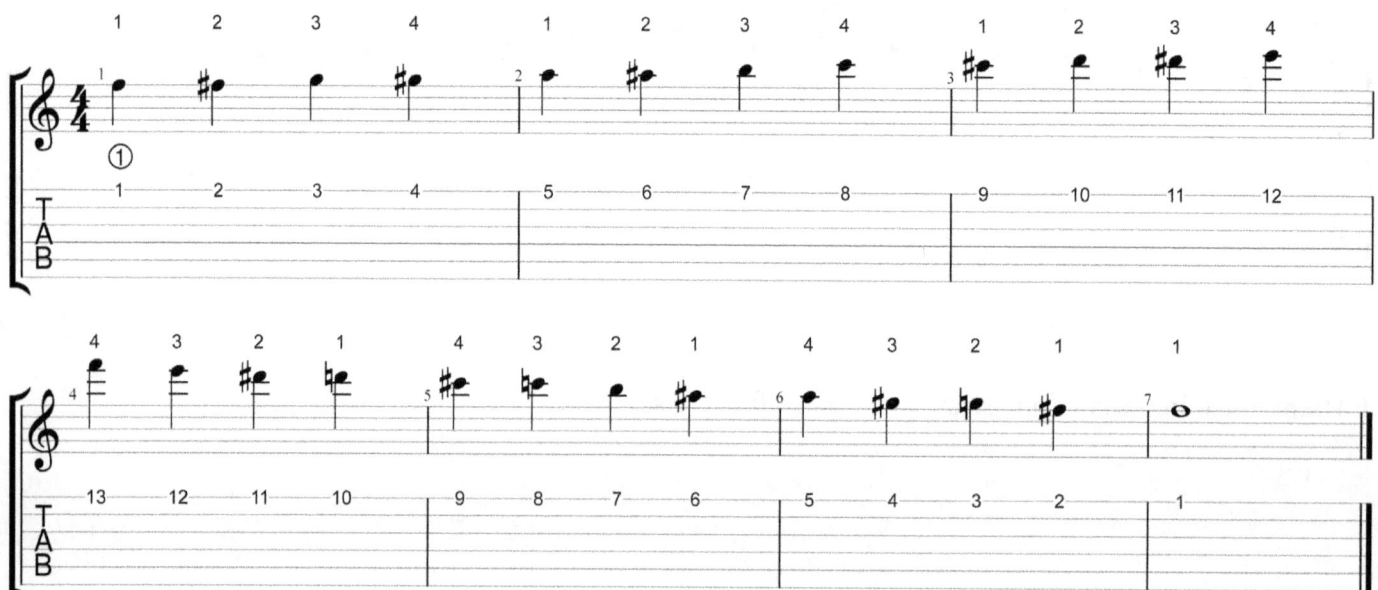

E major scale (one string position shift exercise)

Example 2j

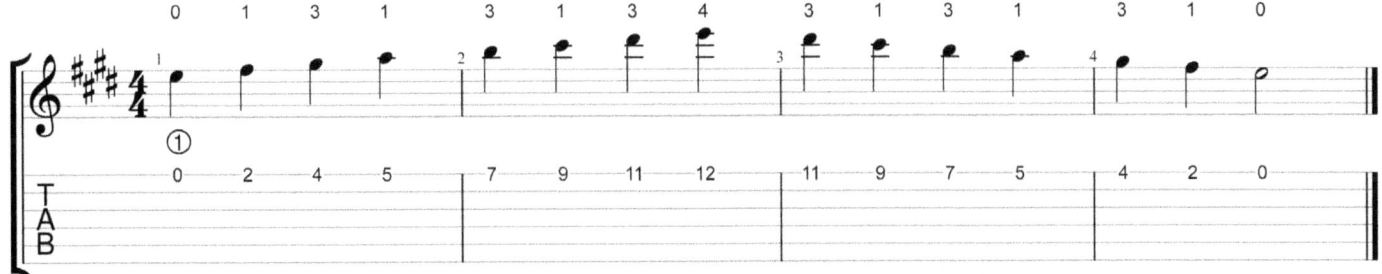

E major scale – alternative fingering (one string position shift exercise)

Example 2k

E natural minor scale (one string position shift exercise)

Example 2l

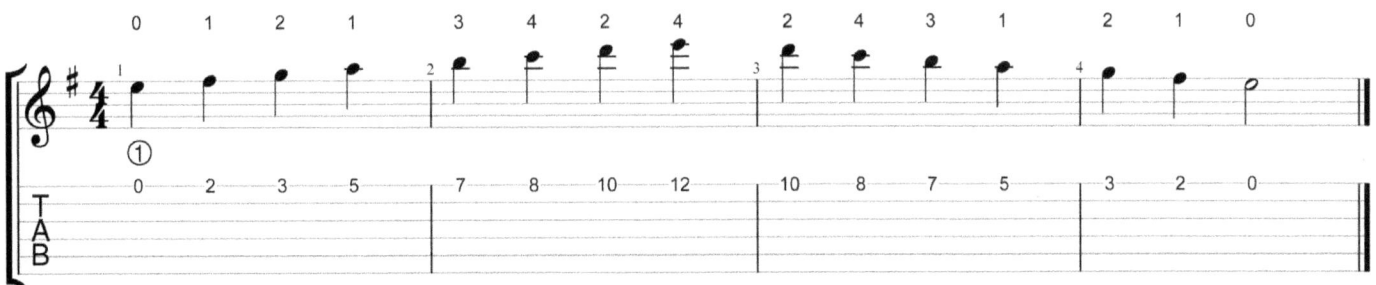

E harmonic minor (one string position shift exercise)

Example 2m

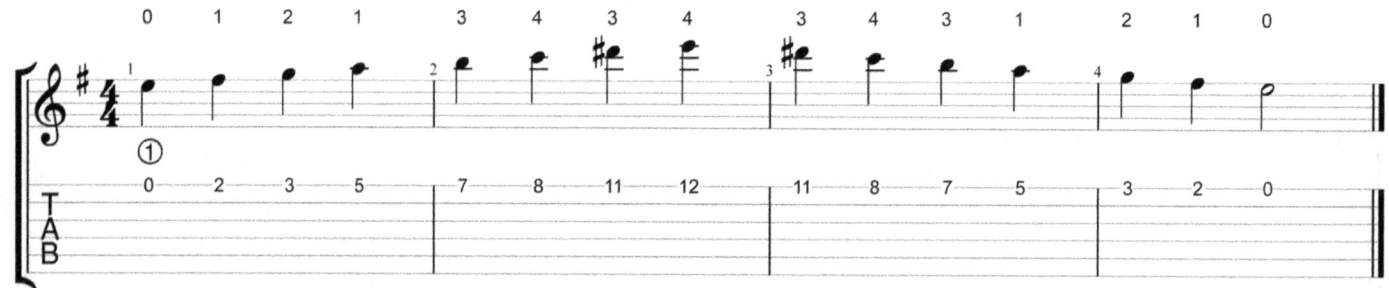

E melodic minor scale (one string position shift exercise)

Example 2n

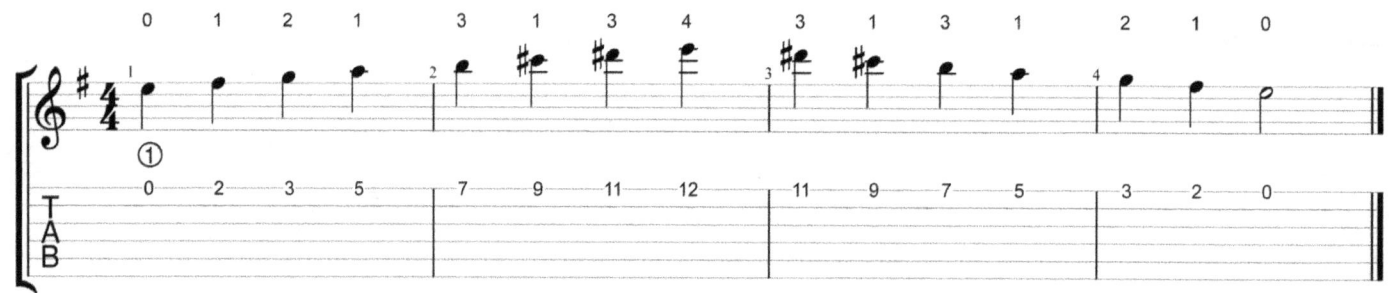

E chromatic scale (one string position shift exercise)

Example 2o

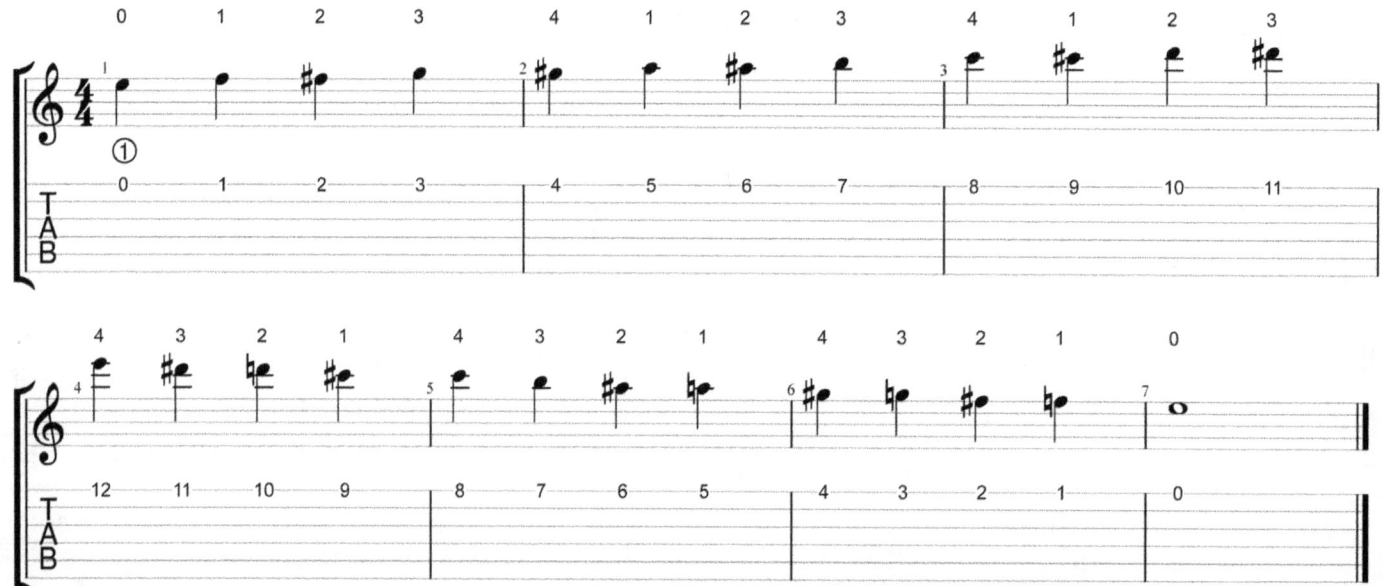

Chapter Three: Legato

In this section we will concentrate on one of the oldest and most common playing techniques, certainly amongst guitar styles: *legato*. It is essential both for the sound it creates and as a way to develop the strength and control of our fretting hand fingers.

Legato is an Italian word meaning *tied* or *bound*. Legato is an articulation technique that allows phrases to have a smooth, continuous flow, with minimum noise while moving from one note to the next. Legato tries to mimic the human singing voice. A singer can transition through multiple notes without having to pause to take a breath to interrupt the sound.

Applied to the guitar, legato means plucking a string once only to play a phrase containing several notes. After the initial pluck, we achieve the sound of each new note in a legato phrase by either:

- Fretting the next note rapidly with a fretting hand finger, with enough force to sound it (commonly known as a *hammer-on*).

- Pulling a fretting hand finger off the string rapidly in such a way that it causes the next note to sound (commonly known as a *pull-off*). The note *pulled-off* to can be an open string or a fretted note that has been previously prepared with another finger.

Inevitably, since *hammer-ons* and *pull-offs* are not played with the same force as a regular stroke over the guitar's resonating chamber, legato passages on the guitar tend to be weaker-sounding than on other instruments. On a violin or cello, for instance, bowing allows for a string's vibration to be sustained at the same intensity for a long time, and legato phrases maintain the same volume throughout. Similarly, blowing air at the same intensity during a phrase allows wind instrument players to create legato phrases without losing volume.

Unamplified plucked instruments such as the guitar are at a disadvantage in this regard. As soon as you pluck a note, it starts to die. The loudest sound occurs immediately after plucking. Therefore, we rely on good technique in our fretting hand to minimise this disadvantage and have good presence in our legato phrases.

It requires a significant amount of finger strength and precision to cause the string to vibrate enough for the sound to have sufficient volume *and* ensure we don't accidentally hit adjacent strings.

When playing the exercises below, keep an eye on the position of your fretting hand and fingers in general. Make sure that you are hitting the strings with the tips of your fingers. This will help you to avoid hitting undesired strings and allow you to use your finger's full strength. Remember to keep your fretting hand thumb behind the neck, without bending the joint. Also ensure that your fingers are positioned in line with the frets (as opposed to on a diagonal angle) and have an arched shape.

These exercises are written to be played in fifth position, but I recommend playing them in all positions as part of your practice routine. Once you get used to the general idea of the exercise, start in first position and move up one position at a time until you get to ninth position (with your little finger working on the twelfth fret). Then descend through all the positions.

Play each exercise on all six strings of the guitar, not just the first. This is important as the feeling of legato playing changes slightly for each string. Tempo is not important to begin with. Monitor your non-playing fingers to make sure you are still keeping them very close to the strings.

Hammer-Ons

Example 3a

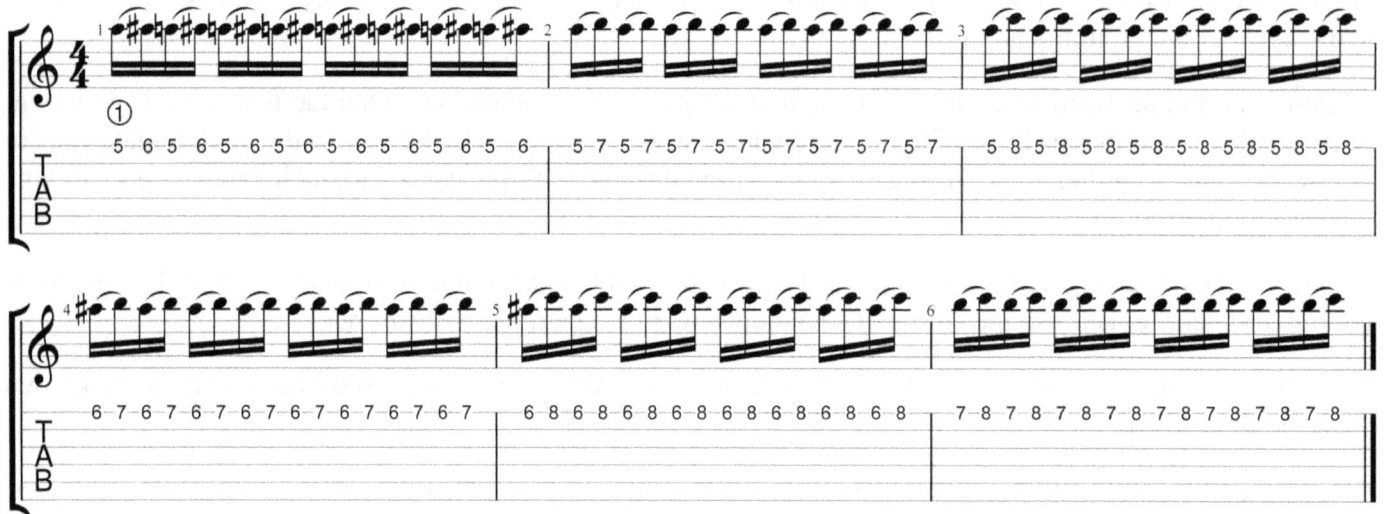

Pull-Offs

A few tips about working on pull-offs that can make your life much easier

It is important with pull-offs to train the fingers to move *as quickly as possible* off the string. The more rapid the movement of the finger leaving the string, the more it will help the string to vibrate freely and produce a louder sound.

In order to help with the task of setting the string in vibration, we pull the finger off and move at a *diagonal* angle. The finger should leave the string and move away from it at an angle of roughly 45 degrees. In this way we produce a *semi-pluck* with the left hand that helps to vibrate the string.

When applying this technique, it is normal to touch the string immediately below the finger that is pulling off, but make sure that you don't accidentally cause it to sound. As you pull off onto a prepared fretted note, you can keep the angle of the finger responsible for pressing this *destination note* very low. This will ensure the string underneath is muted. This is a very important aspect of advanced legato technique!

Example 3b

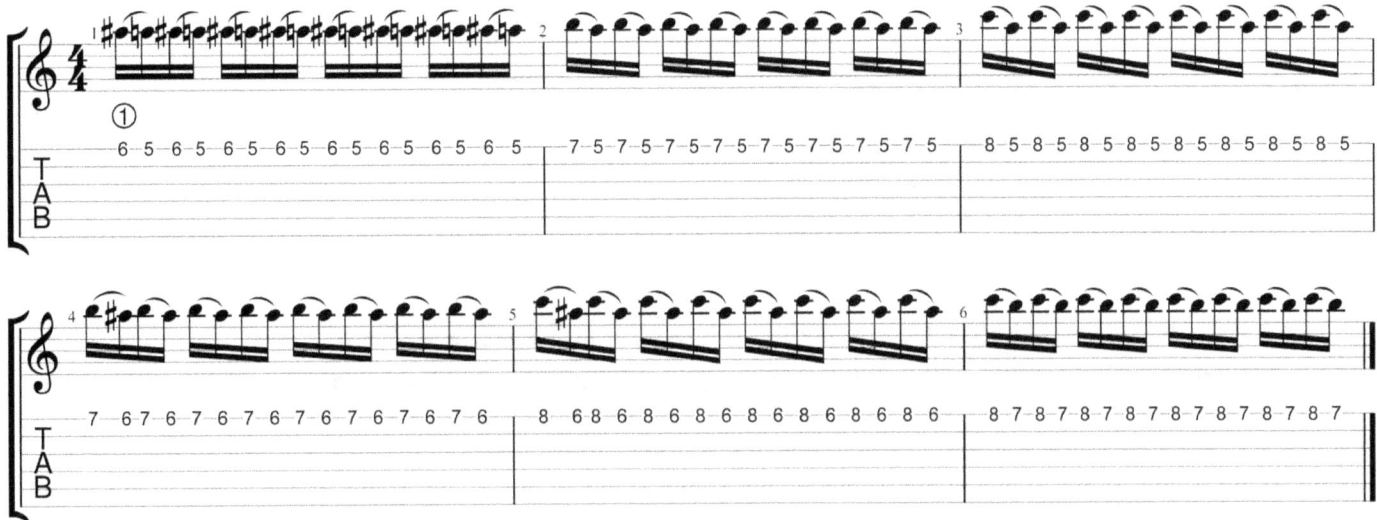

The next two exercises will combine both hammer-ons and and pull-offs. In Example 3c you will play a note and then hammer-on to another, before pulling off to the original note. In Example 3d you will play a note then pull off to another fretted note, before returning to the original note by hammering on. In both, you will be playing three-note phrases with one pluck using legato. The notation shows the exercise in fifth position, but you should take it through positions one through ninth and back, as well as playing it on all strings.

Example 3c

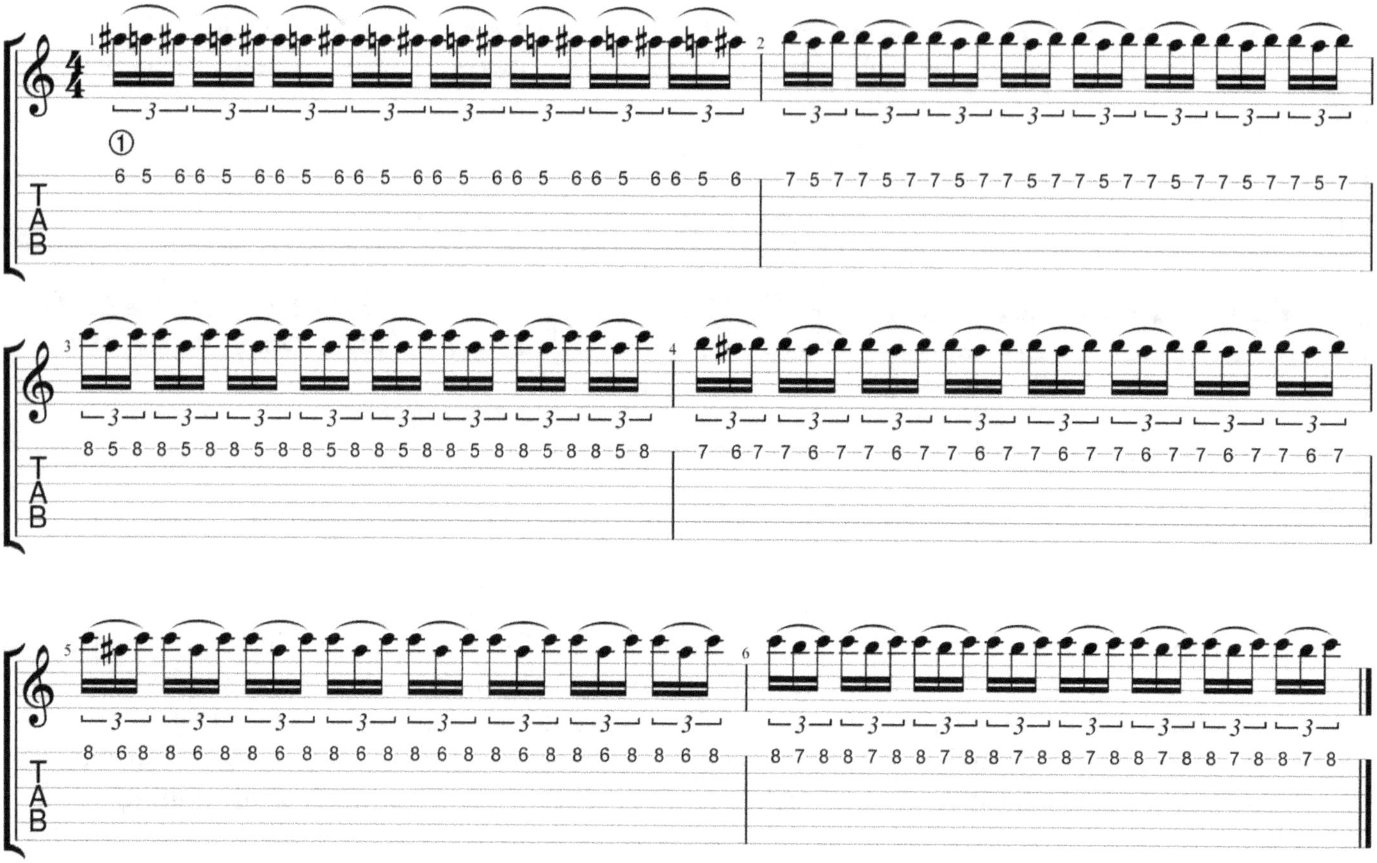

Example 3d

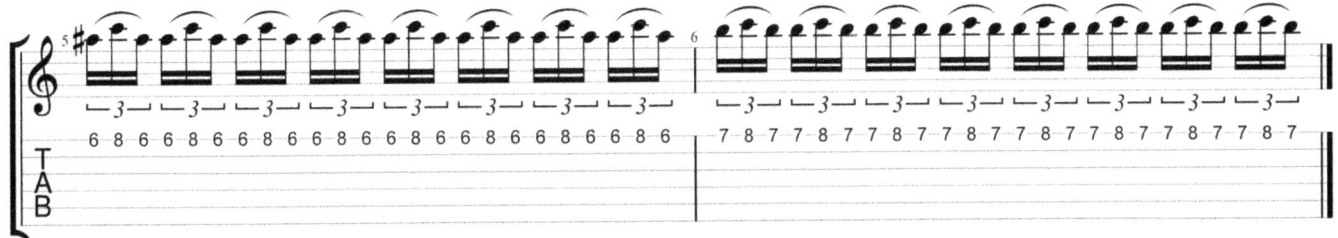

You will now apply legato technique to play position exercises with the E Phrygian Dominant scale. There will be two variations in the fretting hand approach to legato. In the first, you will play two-note legato patterns and in the second you will play predominantly three-note legato patterns.

Both of these are common ways of articulating phrases and it is essential to become accustomed to using them to interpret and learn repertoire. Watch your little finger closely and make sure you keep it close to the strings, following the principles discussed earlier. When we apply a lot of pull-offs, the little finger tends to want to move away from the frets too much!

Example 3e

Example 3f

As you can see, a different approach to legato articulation will make the exact same melodic content sound very different. Indeed, composers, arrangers and interpreters concsiously exploit the expressive possibilities that legato offers when it comes to designing the expressive content of any phrase or piece.

Working without the picking hand

In the following exercises you will not use the picking hand at all. The idea here is to test the legato techniques you have learnt so far, and attempt to produce as much sound from of the instrument as possible (unaided by the picking hand). Practice these two exercises repeatedly over a few weeks, as you continue to work on other exercises. This will help you to monitor your progress in a very effective way.

Example 3g

Example 3h

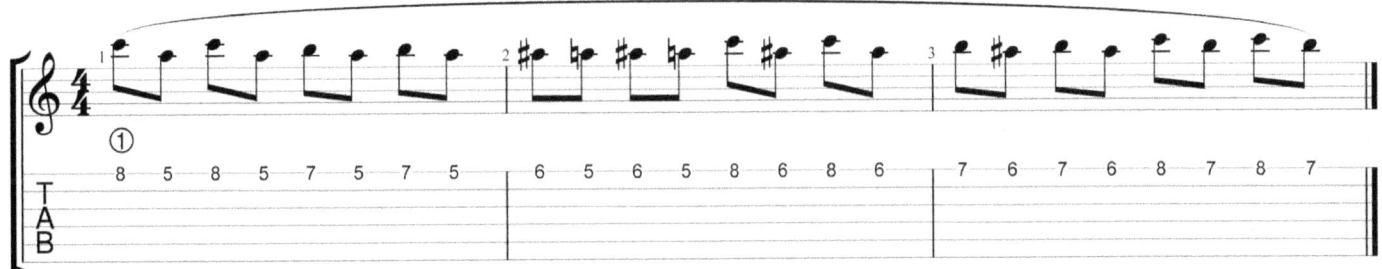

Combining position shifting with legato

Combining position shifting with legato is an important part of classical guitar technique as well as being an essential tool for interpretation. Here, you will revisit some scales played in the position-shifting section, but now you will apply legato technique to them, combining both skills.

The legato patterns included below have been selected with the aim of providing good training at this stage of learning, as well as producing a sound that is pleasing. However, I encourage you to experiment with this technique and also create new patterns from the scales. As you may quickly notice, there are many options!

Remember, position shifting is all about lightness of movement. Play slowly but *move* quickly and visualising the next area you will move into in advance.

F major scale (one string- legato)

Example 3i

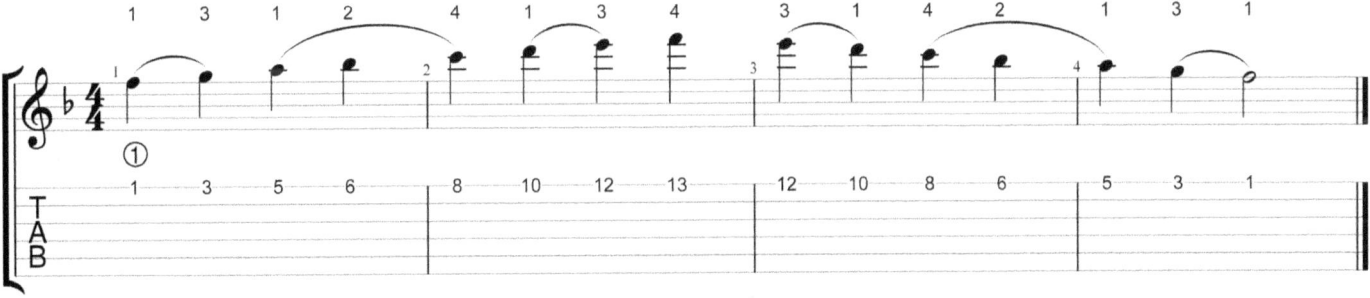

F natural minor scale (one string - legato)

Example 3j

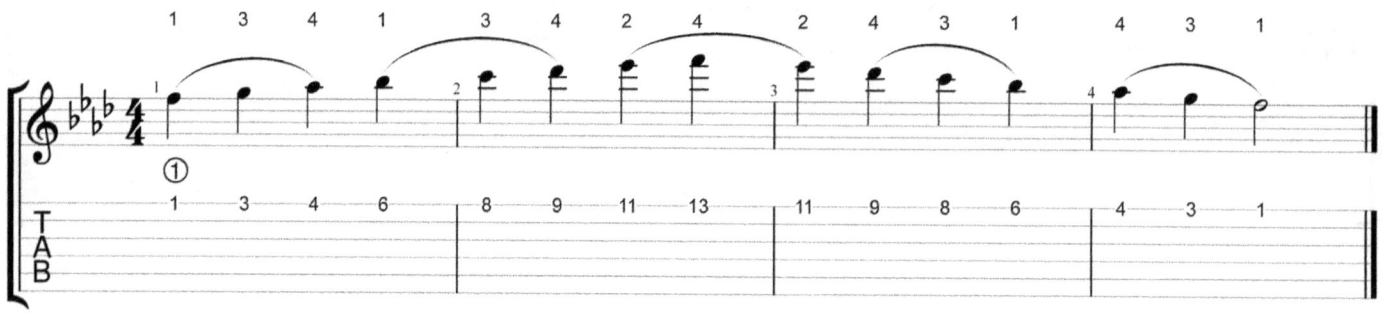

F Harmonic minor scale (one string - legato)

Example 3k

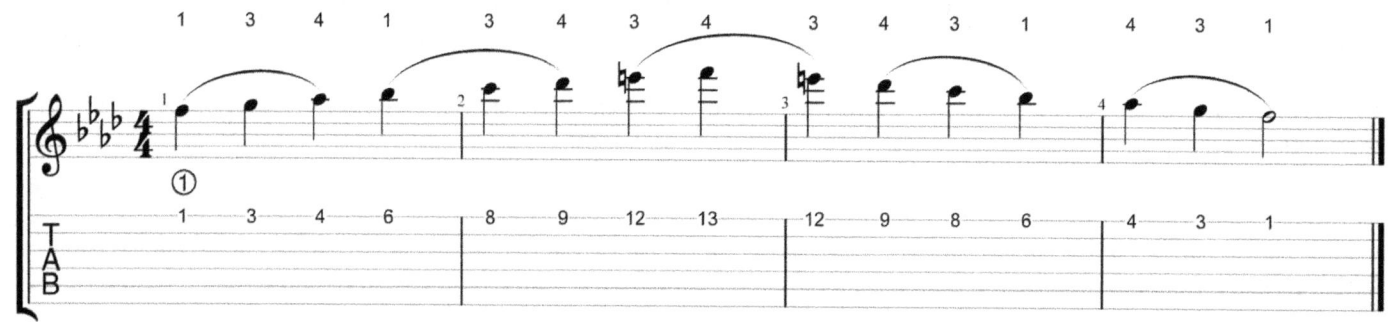

F Melodic minor scale (one string - legato)

Example 3l

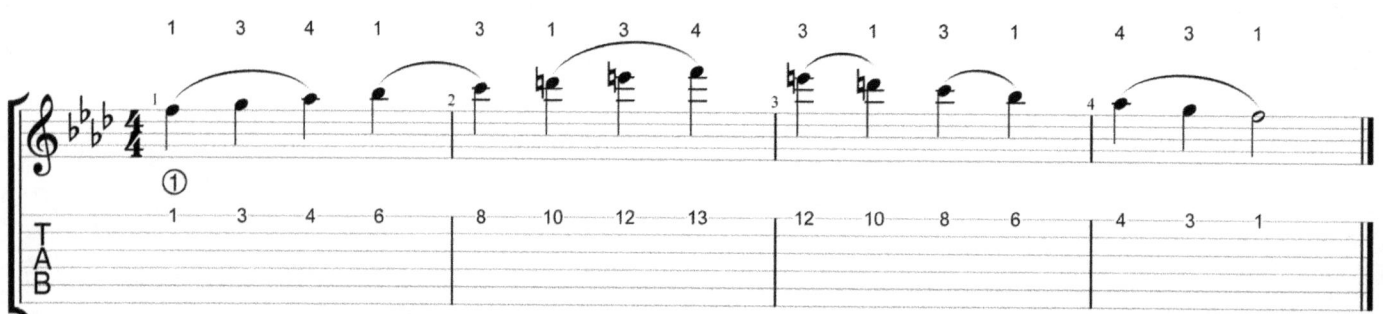

F chromatic scale (one string - legato)

Example 3m

E major scale (one string – legato)

Example 3n

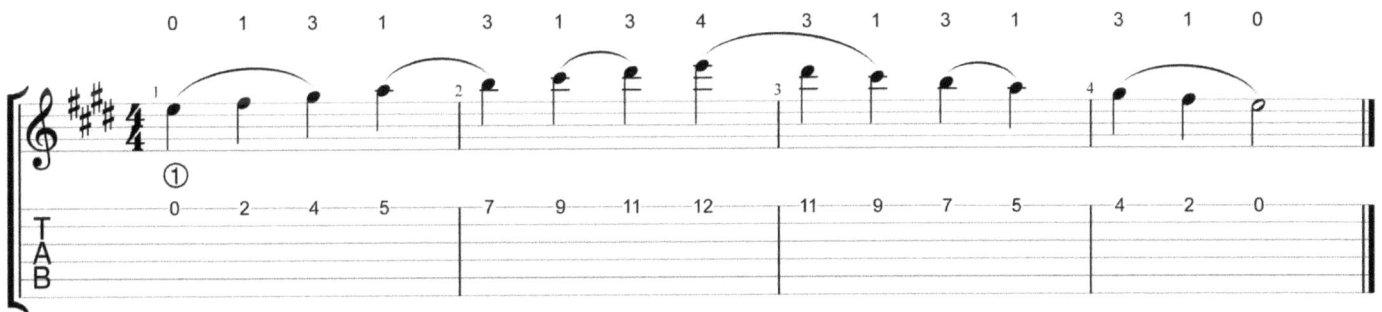

E natural minor scale (one string - legato)

Example 3o

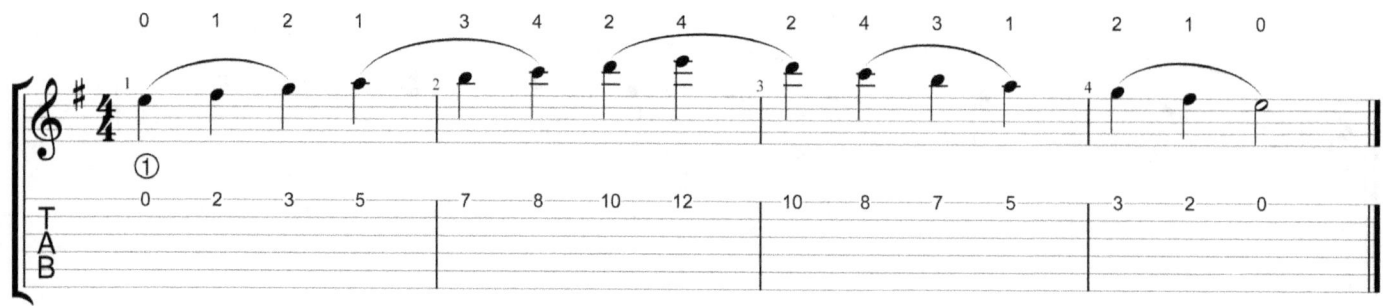

E harmonic minor (one string- legato)

Example 3p

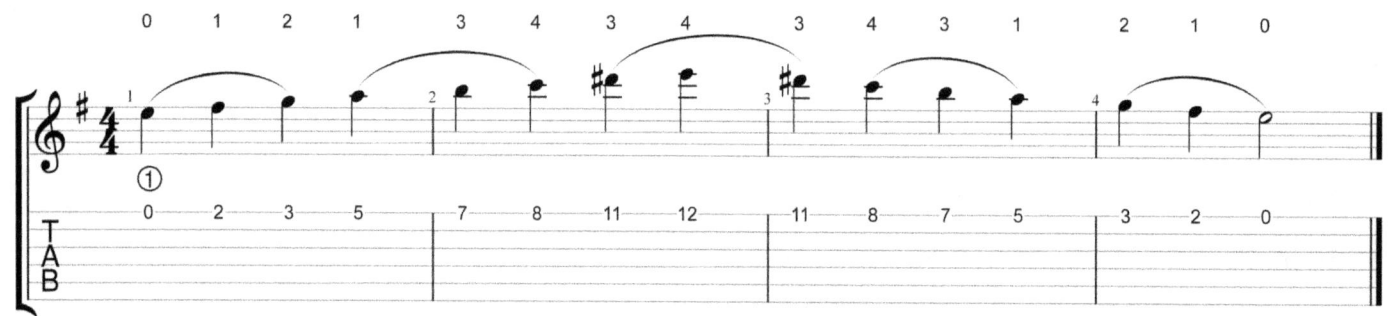

E melodic minor scale (one string – legato)

Example 3q

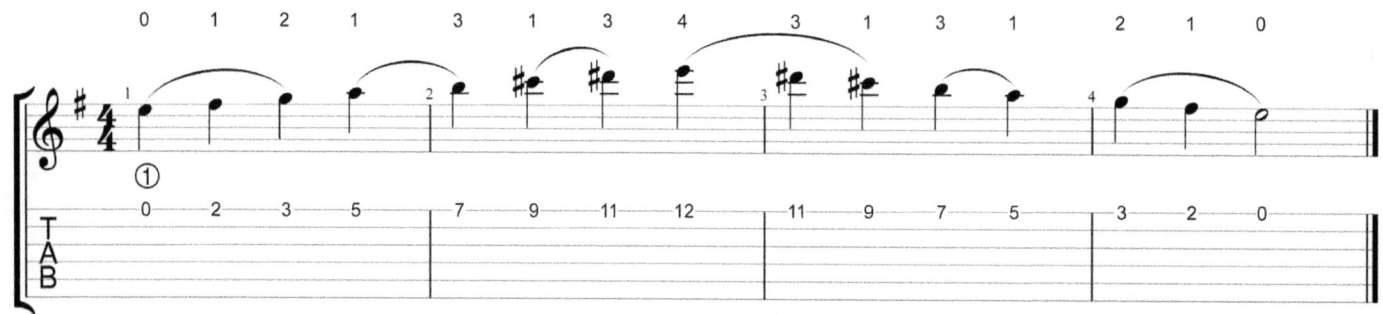

E chromatic scale (one string - legato)

Example 3r

The final exercise in this chapter is an excerpt from J. S. Bach's *Bourree in E Minor*. Some arrangements of this piece don't include the use of legato. However, the natural movement of the upper melody in this section lends itself perfectly to the practice of this technique. Outside of legato practice, the piece itself is a challenging exercise, a masterful piece of writing and a favourite amongst guitarists.

Example 3s

Chapter Four: Developing and Refining Tone with the Picking Hand

Unlike the rest of this book, this chapter is not designed to make your hands and fingers work physically hard! Instead, it is dedicated to another very important aspect of classical guitar technique – one which is absolutely critical as you become more advanced: tone quality and production; plus, understanding the physical characteristics of your instrument and how they affect tone.

Basic philosophy

Andrés Segovia (widely regarded as the most influential classical guitarist and educator of the 20th century) once said, "The guitar is like a little orchestra." His vision was that within his instrument, he could access miniature versions of the different sections of the orchestra. Playing firmly and very close to the bridge would produce a sound similar to that of brass. Playing melodies on the lower strings, close to the sound hole, would emulate the sound of the cello, etc.

Moving between these different tone colours, depending on the characteristics of each passage, will give your playing much greater depth. Cultivating this general mentality is essential and a huge part of what makes an authentic classical guitar sound.

As simple as it may sound at first, this is a long and fascinating subject, with a lot more to learn than first meets the eye. Read on!

As a first exercise on tone and sound colour you will play the following passage twice. The second time you will be instructed to apply a different technical approach in order to compare the sounds produced. First, play it normally as you see it, without considering anything other than the notes you find on the page.

Example 4a

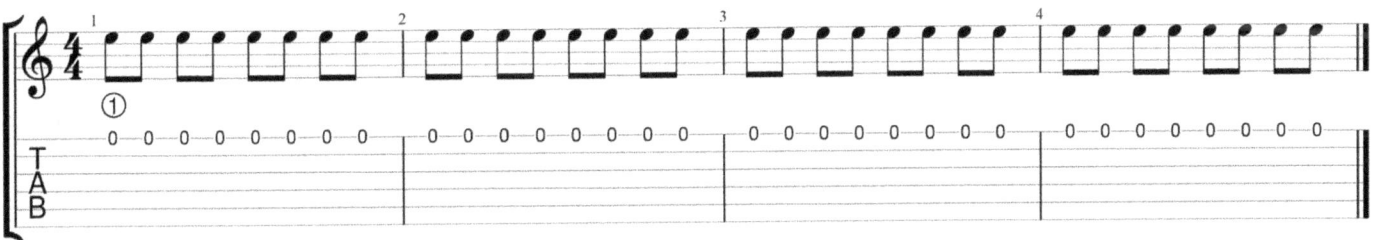

Now, *very slowly,* play Example 4a again. This time, carefully incorporate the following instructions:

- Play the first bar as close to the bridge as you can. With each stroke, gradually rotate the angle with which your nail strokes the string from side to side. Listen carefully.

- As you play the second bar, very gradually move your picking finger towards the sound hole. Continue rotating the angle of your nail from side to side as you play. Listen carefully.

- As you reach the sound hole, keep moving *slowly* towards the neck for the remaining bars, continuing to rotate your nail angle from side to side. Keep listening carefully.

You get the idea. Repeat the steps above moving back and forth between the neck and the bridge and listen intently. If you are paying close attention and doing this slowly (rotating your nail angle) you will hear *very* different sounds coming out of your instrument while playing the same note. Each of these sounds has a use. Applied at the right time, each will provide the perfect tone colour for a passage.

How the strings produce the best tone

In order to be in the best position possible to produce a great tone, it is important to have a basic understanding of how the guitar actually *creates* sound. The sound you hear originates with the vibration of the string. This vibration is transferred onto the body of the guitar (the resonating chamber underneath your picking hand) via the bridge. The bridge is, in fact, the only point of connection between your strings and the resonating chamber of your instrument.

Within the resonating chamber, the upper plate (the front wood board which features the sound hole) plays a critical role in the production of sound. It is this plate vibrating up and down (towards and away from you as you play) which agitates the particles of air around it the most, creating the sound waves that reach our ears. These vibrations are very fast and small, invisible to the human eye.

The principle is: the more the upper plate vibrates, the bigger and richer the sound.

Any vibration on the strings will cause the upper plate to vibrate to some extent. So, how can you help it to vibrate as much as possible? The answer is in the direction in which we set the strings to vibrate when we pluck. If we strike them to vibrate sideways, relative to the body of the guitar, the vibrations of the upper plate will be considerably less than if we cause them to vibrate up and down (towards and away from the upper plate).

You can now prove this with the following exercise. Play the this phrase twice, observe the instructions below each time, then compare the sounds.

The first time:

- Move your picking hand over the fourth fret of the neck (towards the nut of the instrument)
- Keep your hand in that area and use your thumb (p) to pluck your way through the passage, as illustrated below. Listen carefully to the sound. Play *mezzo forte* (with a medium-loud intensity).

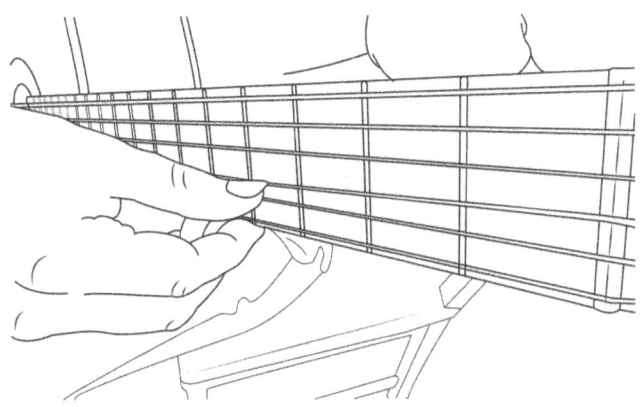

The second time:

- Play the phrase again with the same amount of force, but this time *pinching* the string upwards (outwards) using your thumb (p) and index (i) finger (illustrated below) keeping your hand in the same position. Listen carefully to the sound and compare it with the sound produced before.

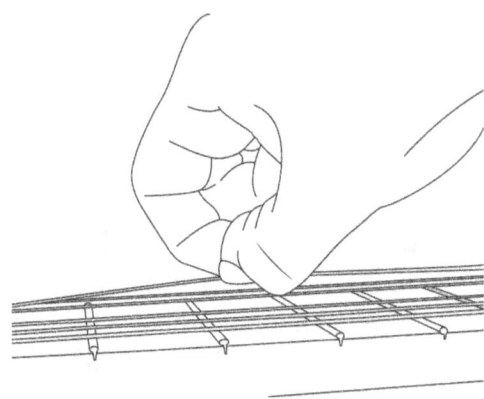

Alternate between the two approaches above and compare the sound. Even though you are using the same amount of force, you should hear significantly more volume produced when you use the *pinching* approach, as well as a deeper, fuller quality to the tone. Because the strings are vibrating up and down (towards and away from the resonating chamber), the upper plate vibrates up and down more than it would otherwise.

As a further and fun exercise to prove this, repeat the two approaches while resting your free hand's fingers *very* lightly as close to the bridge as you can (see image below). Keep your hand in this position while playing the two approaches. You will *feel* significantly more vibration on the upper plate when you apply the *pinching* technique.

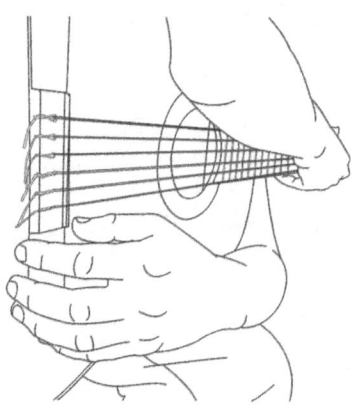

Example 4b

You may be asking yourself why you need to pick the string close to the nut for this experiment. This same process can be tried in your normal picking position. The difference in tone produced will be the same, but you will get a nasty snap sound with it. Why? When you release the string after *pinching* it upwards, it will rapidly undulate downwards and crash against the frets, thus creating that nasty slap sound. When we do it the other way around, it undulates exactly the same way but to the opposite side, where there are no frets for it to crash into.

This of course raises the question: how can it ever be useful to constantly pluck from the wrong end of the guitar? The solution is explained in the following section!

Technical approach to picking for the best tone

We have learnt that in order to produce a rich tone with great presence, the strings need to vibrate towards and away from the acoustic chamber of your guitar. However, conventional, instinctive picking does not cause strings to vibrate in this manner. Instead, it tends to cause them to vibrate towards and away from the floor.

In order to be able to play naturally and also cause the strings to vibrate in the way discussed, you will learn the following technique.

Step one: you need to have nails that have a smooth and continuous outer line, without any cuts or points. They should have an elongated oval shape, which acts as a ramp when plucking, and should be just as long as the (unflattened) end of your finger. All of these characteristics are shown in the image below:

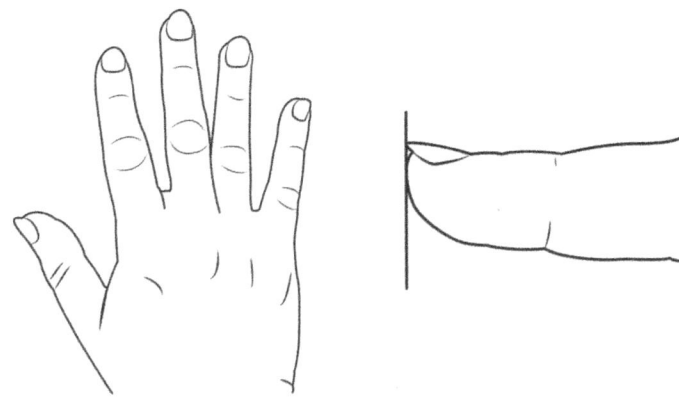

Step two: you need to position your picking fingers to rest on the strings in the neutral playing position. This means: thumb (p) on the sixth (low E) string, index finger (i) on the third (G) string, middle finger (m) on the second (B) string and ring finger (a) on the first (high E) string. The fingers should be just to the right of the sound hole. Place the right-hand edge of your fingernails at an approximately 45-degree angle from the strings. (See the image below as a guide).

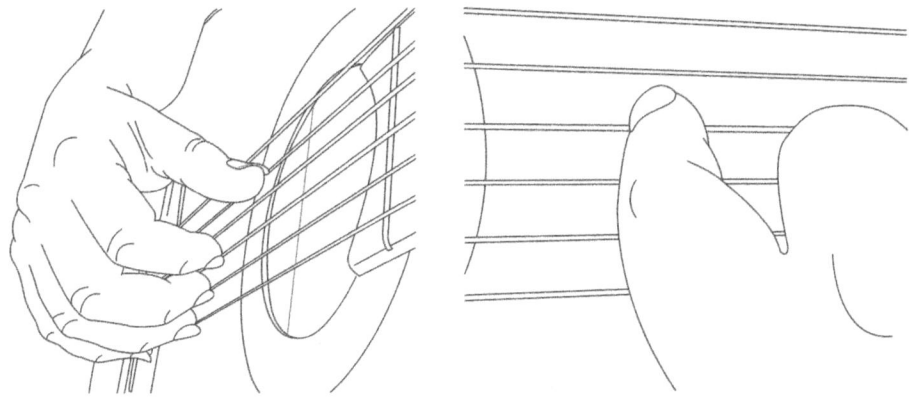

Step 3: with your index finger (i), maintain the 45-degree angle and pluck the third string (G). The stroke must take place from the point where the nail first separates from your finger skin, as shown below. There should be a little bit of skin involved at the start of the stroke, to be followed by the rest of the *nail ramp* (see image below). This helps to produce a warm, refined sound. Additionally, the movement of your finger should originate from the knuckle, as opposed to the smaller joints on the length of the finger. This ensures that you use the full strength of your finger.

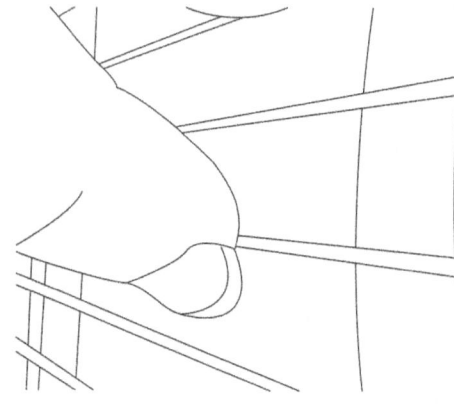

Play this stroke repeatedly and leave a good time interval between each repetition. You should be aiming for a quick movement of the fingernail through the string, to reduce the sound of the stroke and enhance the pure sound of the note. Learning to play this way naturally is, of course, a habit that must be developed with time and patience. The remaining exercises in this chapter will help you to achieve that.

Example 4c

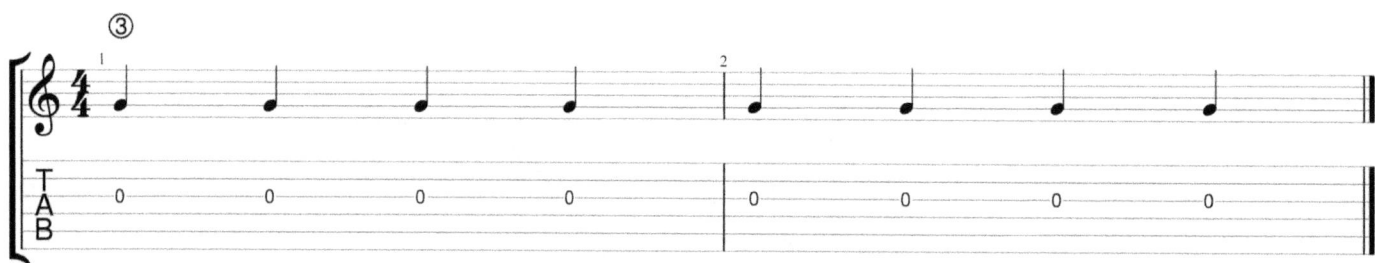

Now, repeat the exact same procedure with your other fingers. Be very patient and give your fingers time to adapt. Over the next several weeks, you should start your practice with a five-to-ten minute warm-up on this technique using the exercises that follow. Although the thumb cannot achieve the same effect on the strings, we should still aim for a very rapid movement of it through the strings, and still have a ramp-shaped nail as per the image above. More guidance on refining the thumb stroke will follow in later chapters.

Things to remember about tone techniques

The above technique must be applied to plucking the strings whether we are playing free strokes (*tirando*: following the stroke by letting the finger move naturally away from the strings after plucking) or rest strokes (*apoyando*: following the stroke by immediately resting your finger on the adjacent string). It is necessary to master both approaches. Single-note melodic lines are usually played with rest strokes (*apoyando*) for deepness of tone, while free strokes (*tirando*) are generally used for arpeggio and chord-based passages, where several strings are required to ring simultaneously.

There are a vast range of tone and colour possibilities available on your instrument. Gradually, as your playing becomes more advanced, they all need to be used to access the expressive qualities of each passage. For now, however, you will focus on getting used to applying a rich, neutral tone.

Tone development routine

Next, you will practice the concepts discussed in this chapter through the following exercises. Don't think about how easy the notes are to play – you are working on developing a big, rich tone. Remember:

- Play from the point of your finger where the nail separates from the skin
- Pluck with a 45-degree angle
- Aim for a rapid follow-through movement past the string
- Ensure that the movement of your picking finger originates from the knuckle of the hand.

For now, use free strokes, as there will be more work on rest strokes later in the book.

Example 4d

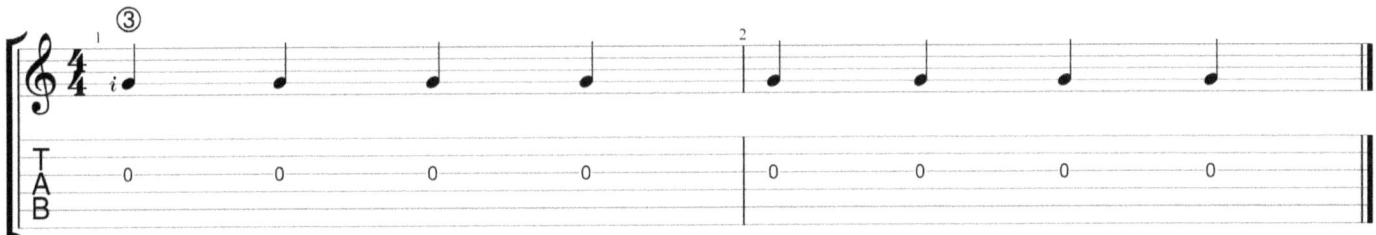

Example 4e

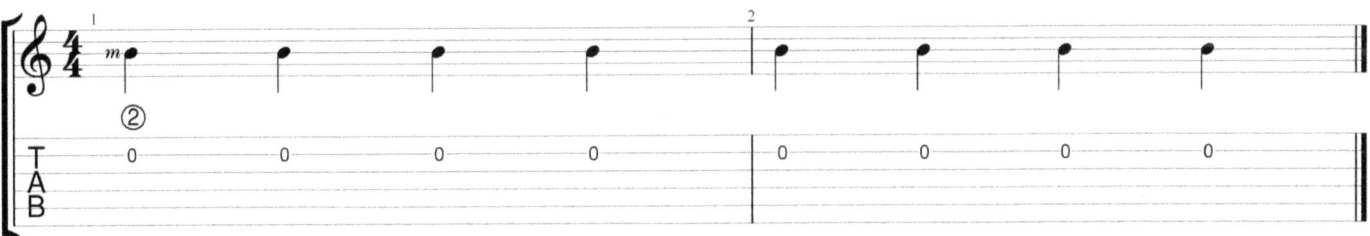

Example 4f

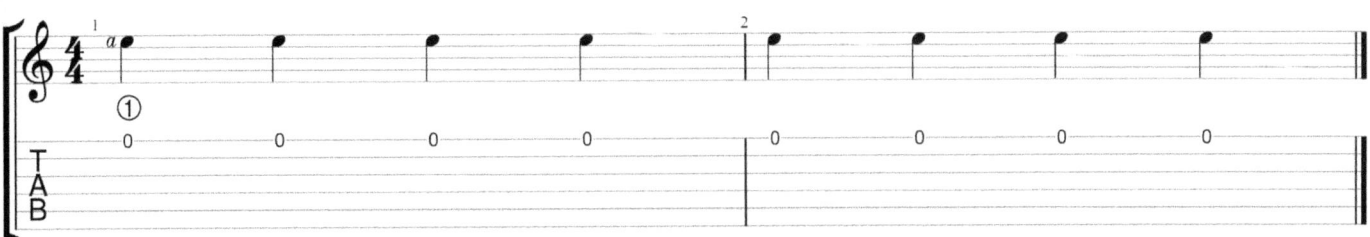

Example 4g

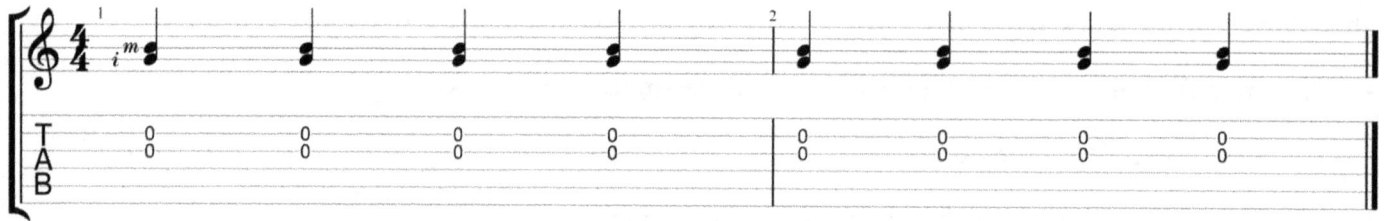

Example 4h

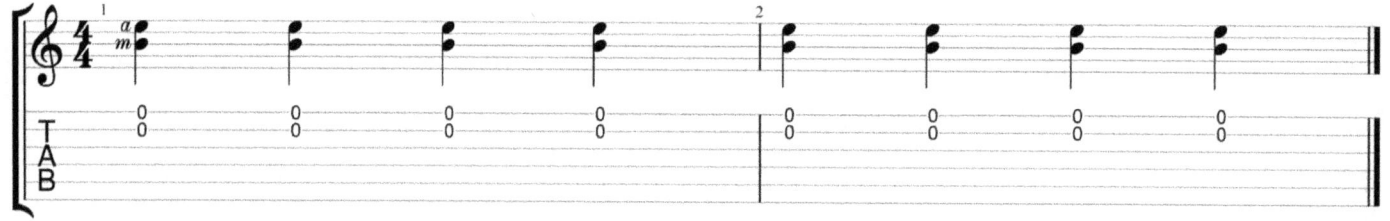

Example 4i

(figure)

Example 4j

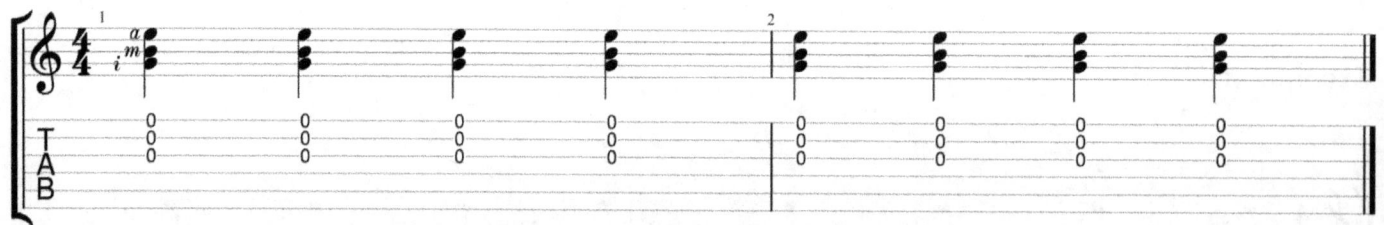

Example 4k

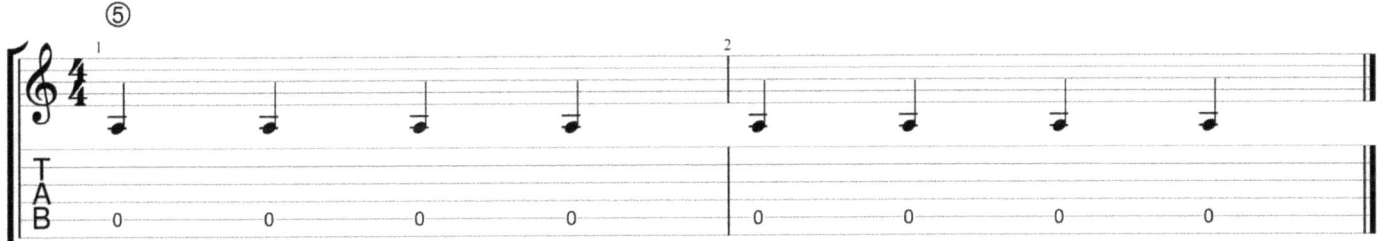

Example 4l

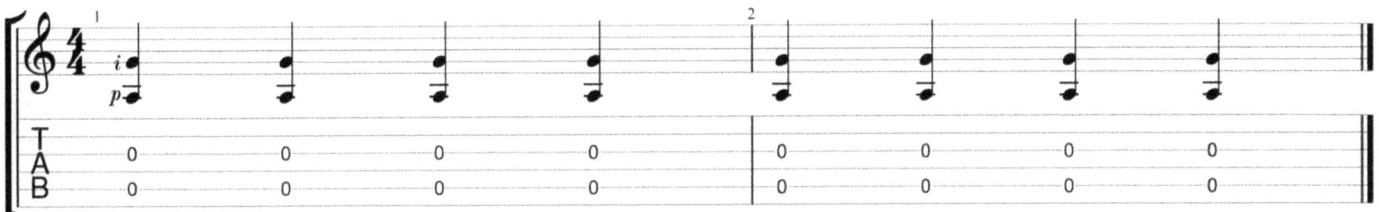

Example 4m

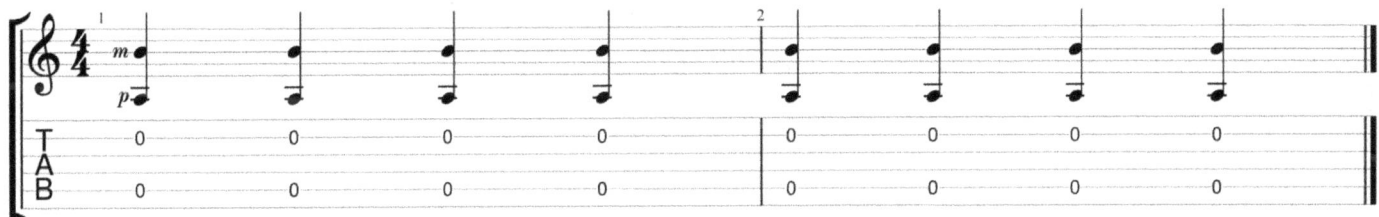

Example 4n

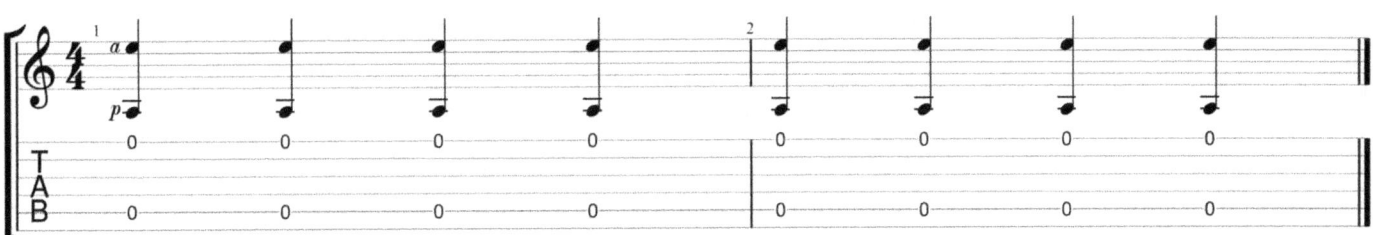

Example 4o

Example 4p

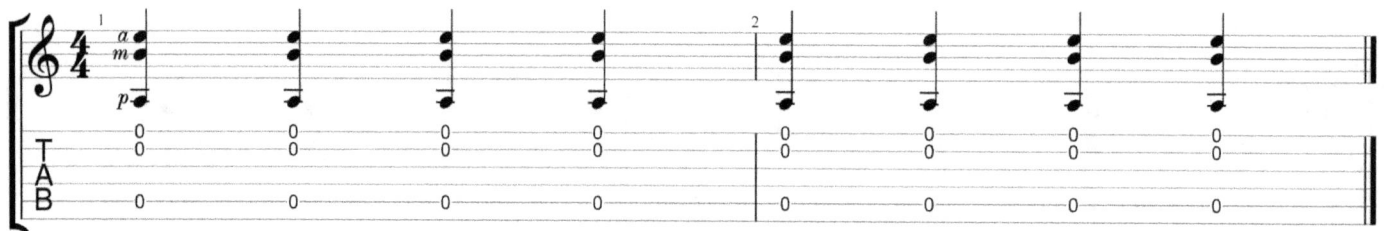

Example 4q

Example 4r

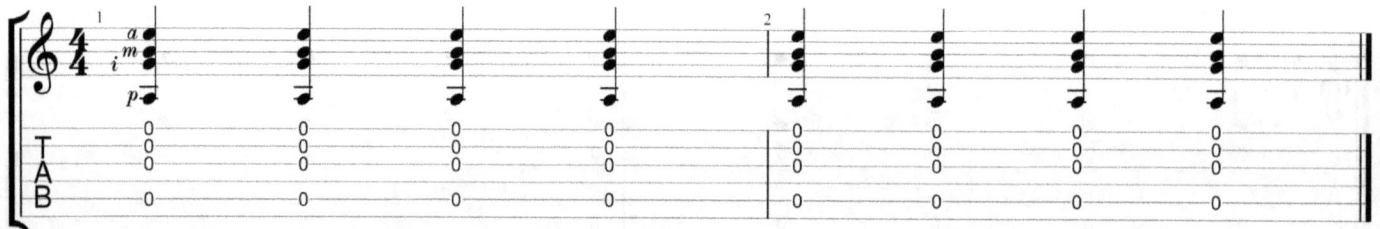

To complete this chapter, you will start to apply the tone production techniques you've learned to musical phrases in a simple study. For the purpose of this exercise, continue to use free strokes. However, remember that you should apply these techniques to all of your playing and to the remaining material in this book.

Example 4s

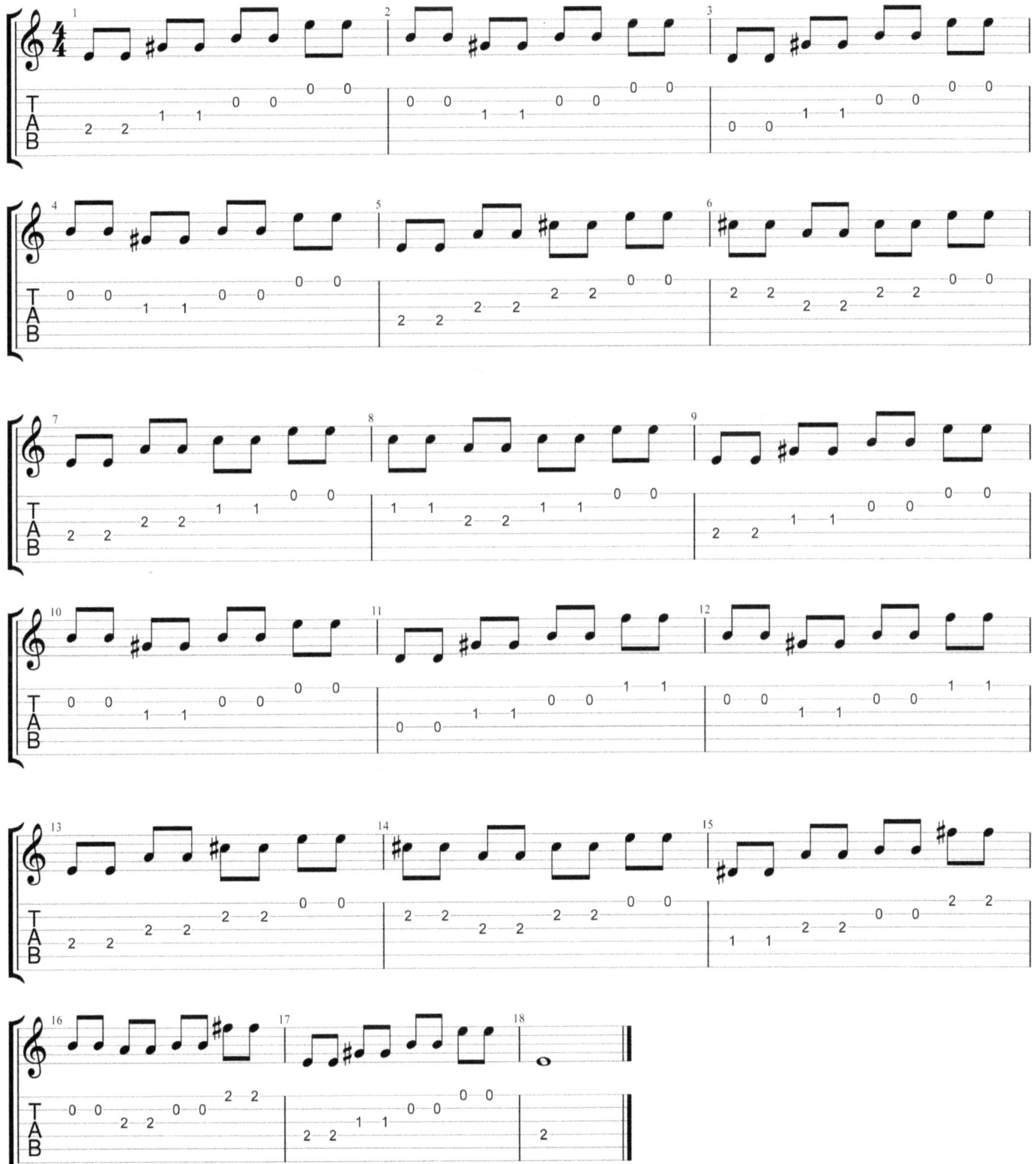

Chapter Five: Arpeggio Playing

In this chapter you will focus on one of the most essential techniques for any classical guitarist: playing arpeggios. The word *arpeggio* is Italian in origin. *Arpa* means "harp" in Italian and *arpeggiare* means "to play the harp". This technique is based on the concept of playing a chord or harmony *in the style of a harp*, one note after the other, in a continuous flow.

As a stringed instrument, the guitar lends itself well to the use of arpeggios and can imitate the sound of the harp. The notes of a given held chord can be left to ring simultaneously until the vibration of the strings stops, or until the musical phrase forces the fingers to move on. In order to do this, we need to use free strokes at all times. Note, however, that the term *arpeggio* in modern terminology can also mean to play the notes of the broken chord *without* letting them ring. This occurs most often when arpeggios are played as scale-like patterns, rather than held chord shapes.

In classical guitar repertoire we encounter far more phrases based on *resonating* arpeggios. Since this genre of guitar music contains predominantly solo pieces, the effect of two or more strings ringing together after being plucked separately helps the music sound grander and multidimensional. For this reason, classical guitarists must develop the technique to play *ringing* arpeggios and the ability to play complicated patterns with this technique.

As you play the following exercises, constantly remind yourself of the principles learnt in the previous tone-production chapter. You need to use them continuously in order to develop technique and for them to have a long-lasting impact on your playing.

Ascending and descending chord arpeggios

First, it is important to get your fingers and thumb used to moving in perfect order (ascending: p, i, m, a. Descending: a, m, i, p). You will be applying free strokes to the following exercises. Start very slow, concentrating on playing the exercise properly, then gradually play at a faster tempo. It is critical that you follow the picking hand fingering indications for every exercise in this chapter, so that you really benefit from them.

Example 5a

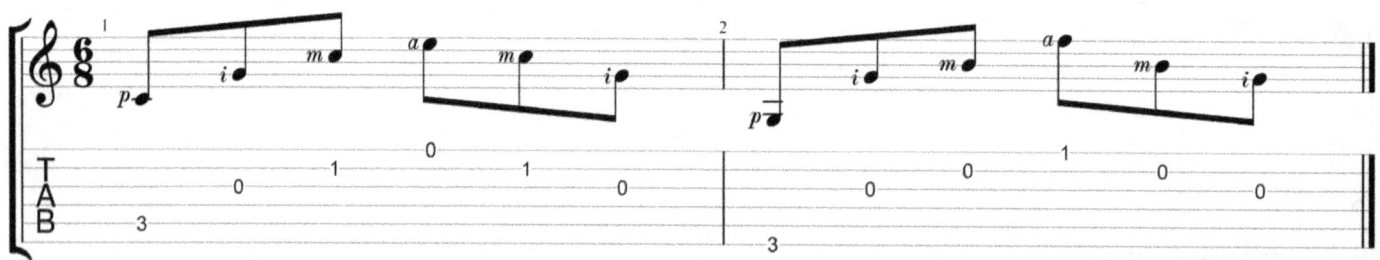

The ascending / descending picking pattern you have just played is one of the most commonly used. Repeat it with several chord patterns in order to get your fingers fully accustomed to using it. Here are some further examples to help you to achieve this. If you know any particular chord sequences that you like, apply it to them too for further practice!

Example 5b

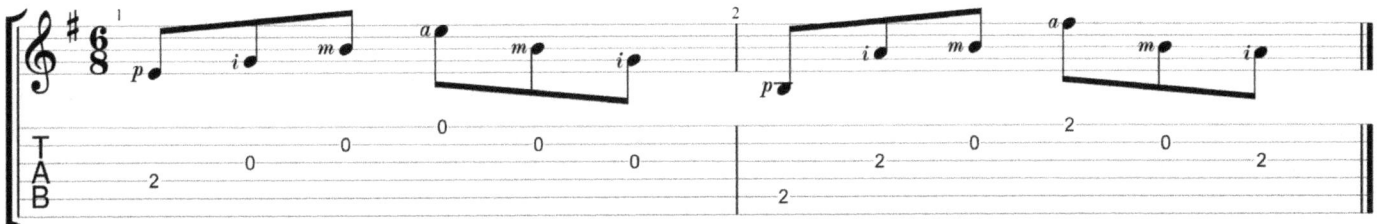

Example 5c

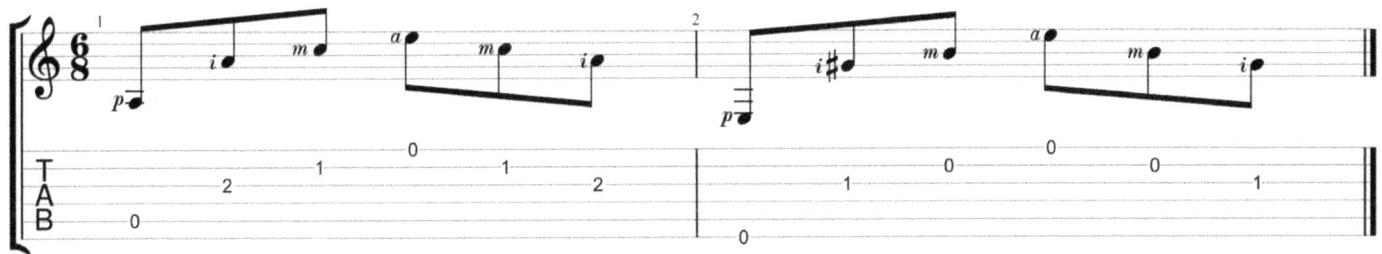

Example 5d

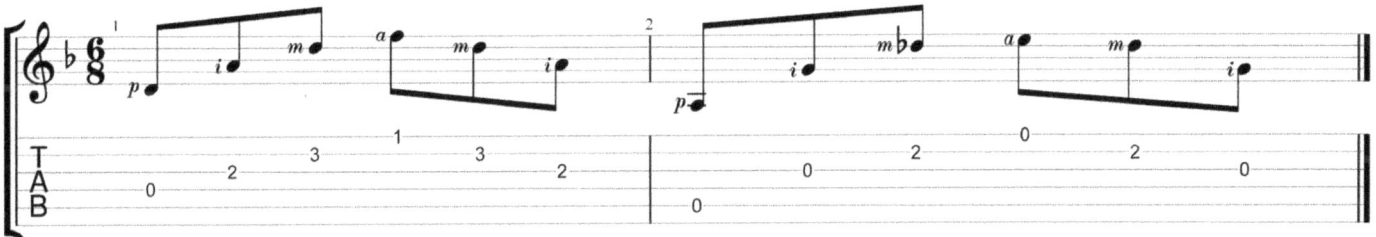

Example 5e

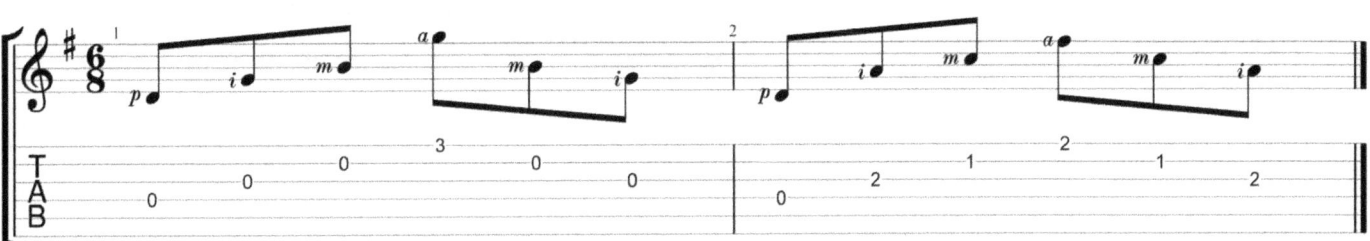

From this point onwards, you will work on getting your fingers to move in ways which require more independence. As you play the exercises that follow, monitor the movement of your fingers and thumb closely. Ensure that as soon as any finger strokes a string, it immediately moves towards the next note it will have to play, without stopping or rushing. In many cases, this will mean repositioning to play the same note again. This is good preparation that allows the response of the fingers to improve. It will help you to play arpeggio passages faster with fewer issues. If this technique is being executed well, all fingers will be constantly moving (either to play or to reposition themselves). There should be no abrupt movements, with each finger and thumb moving at the minimum speed necessary to play at any given tempo.

Example 5f

Example 5g

Example 5h

Example 5i

Repeat the exercise above with the following variation on the picking hand fingers.

Example 5j

Example 5k

Example 5l

Example 5m

The following arpeggio exercises were written by Francisco Tarrega (arguably the most influential classical guitarist of the 19th century). His work was of immense importance in the development of a refined technique for the classical guitar and his vision still heavily influences the tuition of the instrument today. Additionally, as a composer of repertoire for the genre, he is one of the most celebrated. Tarrega was a great believer in the idea of reversing the combination of fingers used to pluck phrases as a way to develop independence and response. To illustrate this idea, here is an example of one of his simpler arpeggio exercises:

Example 5n

Below are some of the more demanding arpeggio exercises from Tarrega's technical studies. They are a great way of complementing your arpeggio practice and the development of finger independence for the picking hand. Don't rush your way through them. As always, each should sound good and feel comfortable before you move on!

The first four exercises will make you work on using different fingers when playing consecutive notes on the same string. Once developed, the ability to do this allows for much greater fluidity and speed. You will also save energy when playing these kinds of phrases (which are common in advanced repertoire) as you spread the work load across a number of fingers, giving each finger more time to relocate before having to pluck again.

Example 5o

Example 5p

Example 5q

Example 5r

The next four Tarrega arpeggio exercises combine all the fingers and thumb again, this time over a series of triplets. The intricacy of the finger patterns can prove challenging. As with the previous exercises, they are played on open strings, so you can afford to concentrate completely on the picking hand. Allow yourself to watch the picking hand continuously as you play, and concentrate on achieving a constant, non-abrupt movement and *cycling* of each finger.

Example 5s

Example 5t

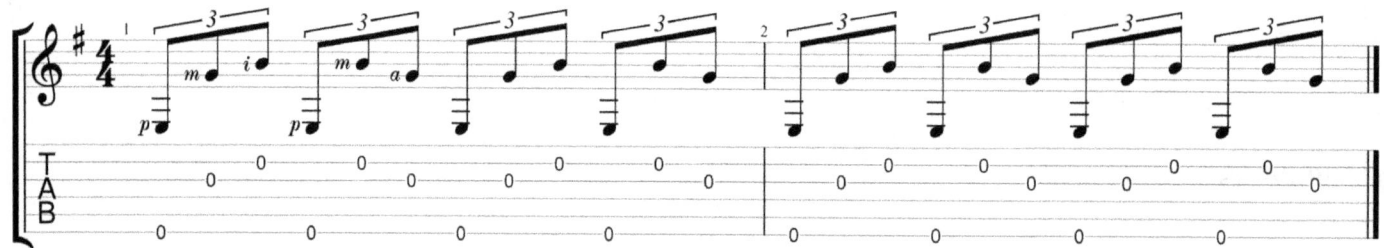

Example 5u

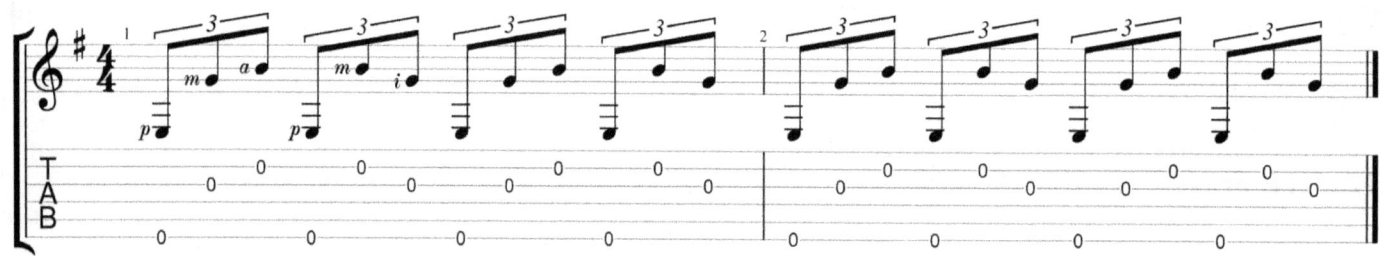

Example 5v

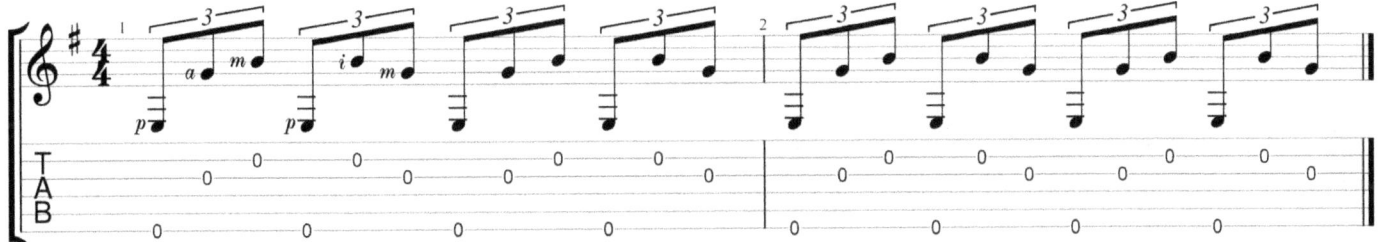

Finger rotation

Often, when playing repertoire, you will find fast, long arpeggio phrases with more than four or five continuous ascending / descending notes. You should always avoid using the same finger to pick two or more notes in succession, particularly when the tempo is quick. In order to tackle such arpeggios, *rotate* your fingers in a logical manner, following the same pattern, to give each finger the same amount of resting time between each stroke. This is hard to develop but, once achieved, allows for a smooth flow of movement between all fingers.

At times during the exercises that follow, you will be required to pluck two consecutive notes on the same string with different fingers. This can be challenging, so spend some time repeating sections where the fingers need to momentarily transition from rotating through different strings to rotating on one.

Example 5w

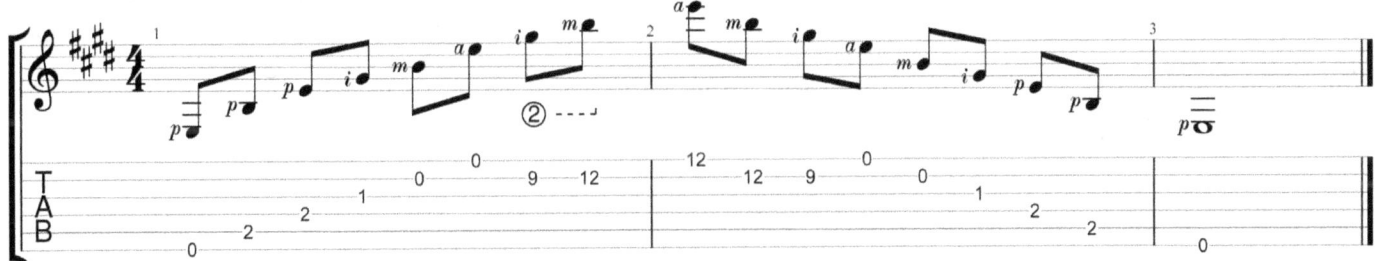

Example 5x

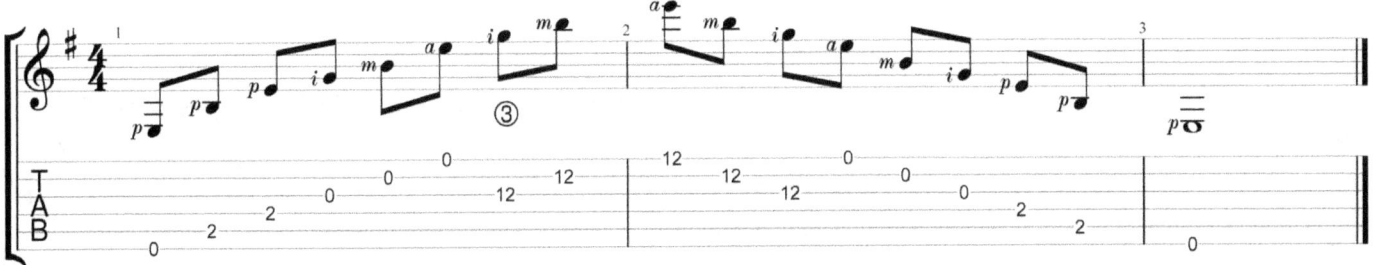

The following example is taken from Brazilian composer Heitor Villa-Lobos's famous *Prelude No.1 in E Minor*.

Example 5y

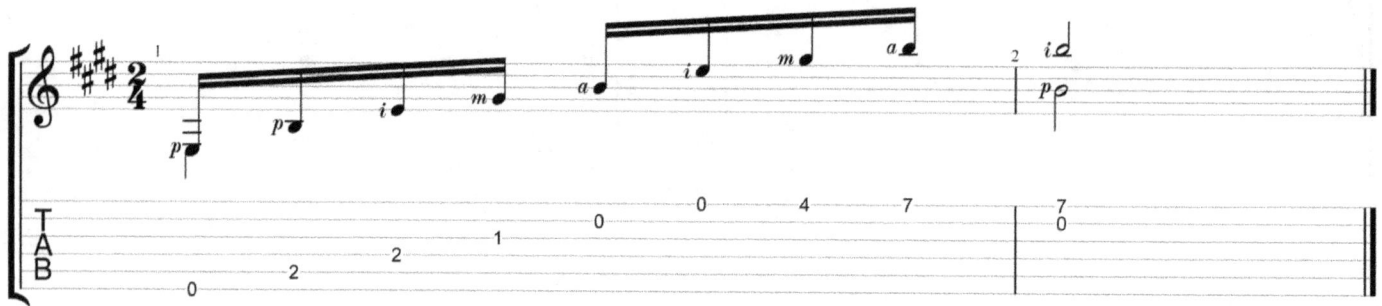

The final arpeggio exercise is by the famous Italian guitarist and educator Ferdinando Carulli. As with many of his studies, it is highly beneficial for practice and also works as a simple, yet very graceful piece of music.

The nature of the arpeggios used serves the purpose of practicing different fingerings on the picking hand. The exercise consists of four sections. In the first two sections, I have intentionally included some *suggestions* on the score which are not the most obvious fingerings many guitarists would instinctively use for the purpose of playing through it in the easiest way possible. I did this in order to get the ring (*a*) finger to do more work. This is a finger that takes more effort to get to respond than the others. This makes the suggested arpeggio fingering pattern for the first two sections: *p, m, a, m*.

However, learn this study both with the written fingering and the more obvious *p, i, m, i*. This will maximise the benefit of the exercise. Additionally, make sure to follow all the suggestions on the third and fourth sections as far as picking hand fingers are concerned. Always repeat them the exact same way if the phrase reappears later in the piece.

Example 5z Ferdinando Carulli Study

Chapter Six: Rapid Arpeggio Patterns

A simple variation on arpeggios

The guitar offers multiple possibilities when it comes to textures and colours. An interesting variation to regular arpeggio playing is when three-note patterns are played *rapidly* in succession, ascending or descending. Although there is nothing different in principle between this and normal arpeggio playing, the velocity of the plucking creates a different kind of sound effect to the regular approach. Because of the speed, it is harder to distinguish the notes clearly, but the almost strum-like sound produced creates a beautiful harmonic background.

There are many similarities between this way of playing arpeggios and *tremolo*, which will be discussed in a later chapter. (Many approaches are simply variations of the same general technique, and many methods teach elements of tremolo within arpeggio studies and vice versa).

To illustrate the idea of a rapid three-note arpeggio, play the exercise below. Notice the richness of sound produced by the quick succession of notes. The key is to strive to produce *even* spacing between the notes, as well as equal accents. Play slowly at first, as for a regular arpeggio exercise, then gradually speed up to an *allegro* tempo.

Example 6a

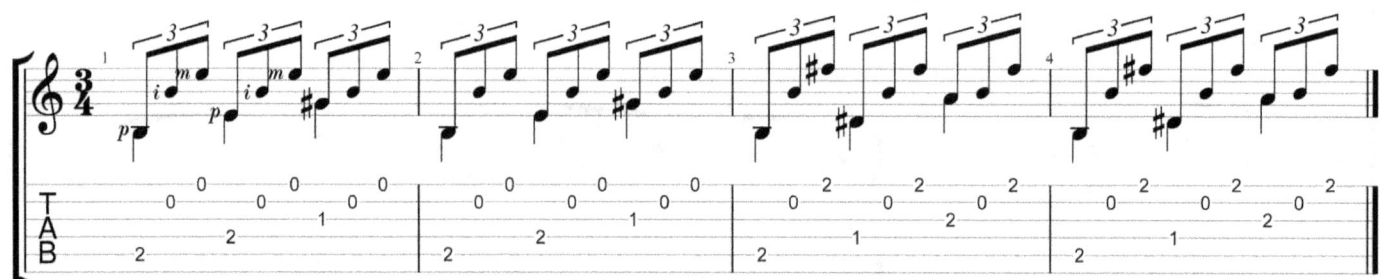

Play the example above using the following finger patterns:

p, m, a, p, m, a, etc

p, i, a, p, i, a, etc

Once the pattern above can be played evenly at a fast tempo, the sound produced is more like an *effect* than a regular melody.

Next are some common variations on the same idea, all of which are brilliant ways to train your fingers to respond faster and move in perfect synchronisation.

Example 6b

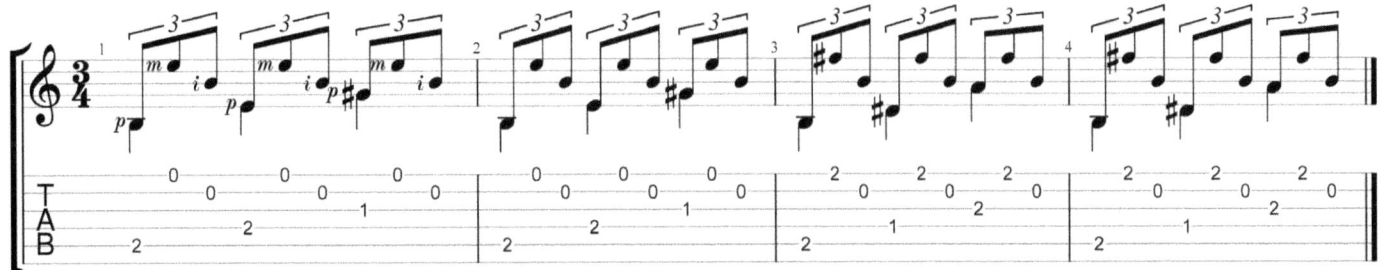

Also play the example above with the following finger patterns:

p, a, m, p, a, m, etc

p, a, i, p, a, i, etc

Example 6c

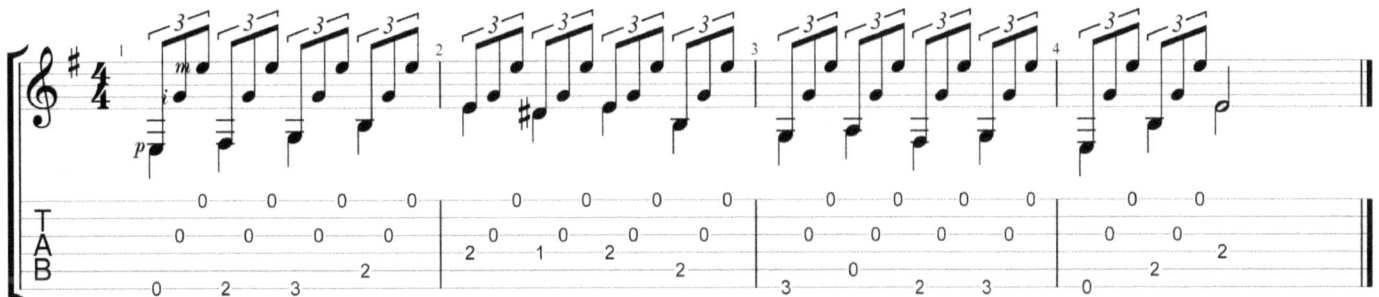

Also play the example above with the following finger patterns:

p, m, a, p, m, a, etc

p, i, a, p, i, a, etc

Example 6d

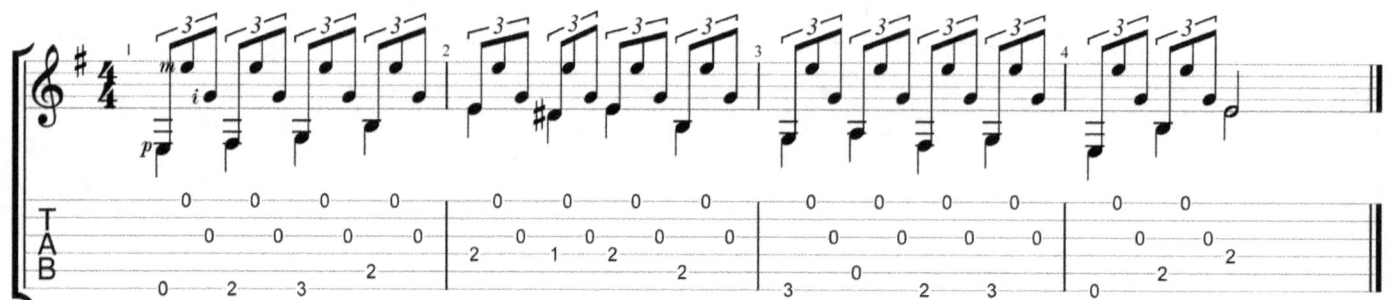

Also play the example above with the following finger patterns:

p, a, m, p, a, m, etc

p, a, i, p, a, i, etc

Four-note rapid arpeggio patterns

The following examples are similar *rapid* arpeggio patterns, but have four notes.

Example 6e

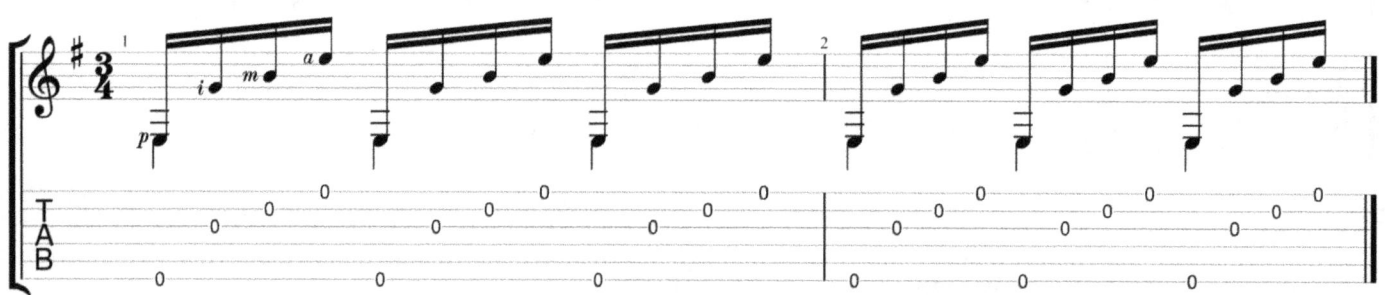

Example 6f

Maintaining balance while moving up and down the fretboard

Playing passages like the ones in this chapter requires a lot of balance and stamina. The space between the strings is small and great precision is needed. A common issue is that movement on the fretboard caused by the fretting hand will throw the strings out of alignment with the picking fingers, affecting the precision of our playing. Work on the following two passages to practice keeping the fretboard as still as possible while moving the fretting hand considerably. Keep an eye on your general posture to help you with this. Don't hold the guitar too tight, but make sure it doesn't move much at all!

Example 6g

Example 6h

"Torre Bermeja"

Here is a passage from the opening section of the piece *Torre Bermeja* by the famous romantic composer Isaac Albeniz. It is a challenging exercise that uses the technique you have been working on in this chapter, as well as being rich with musical beauty. It also incorporates quick position changes in the fretting hand as an extra challenge.

Albeniz's pieces were originally written for piano and inspired by the sound of Flamenco and Spanish guitar music. As it turns out, these pieces were later transcribed for the classical guitar and, to this day, remain some of the most well-known repertoire for the instrument. Curiously, he is responsible for writing on and for the piano, what is arguably the most well-known piece for classical guitar, *Asturias (La Leyenda)*.

Exercise 6i

DADGBE (Tune 6 down to D)

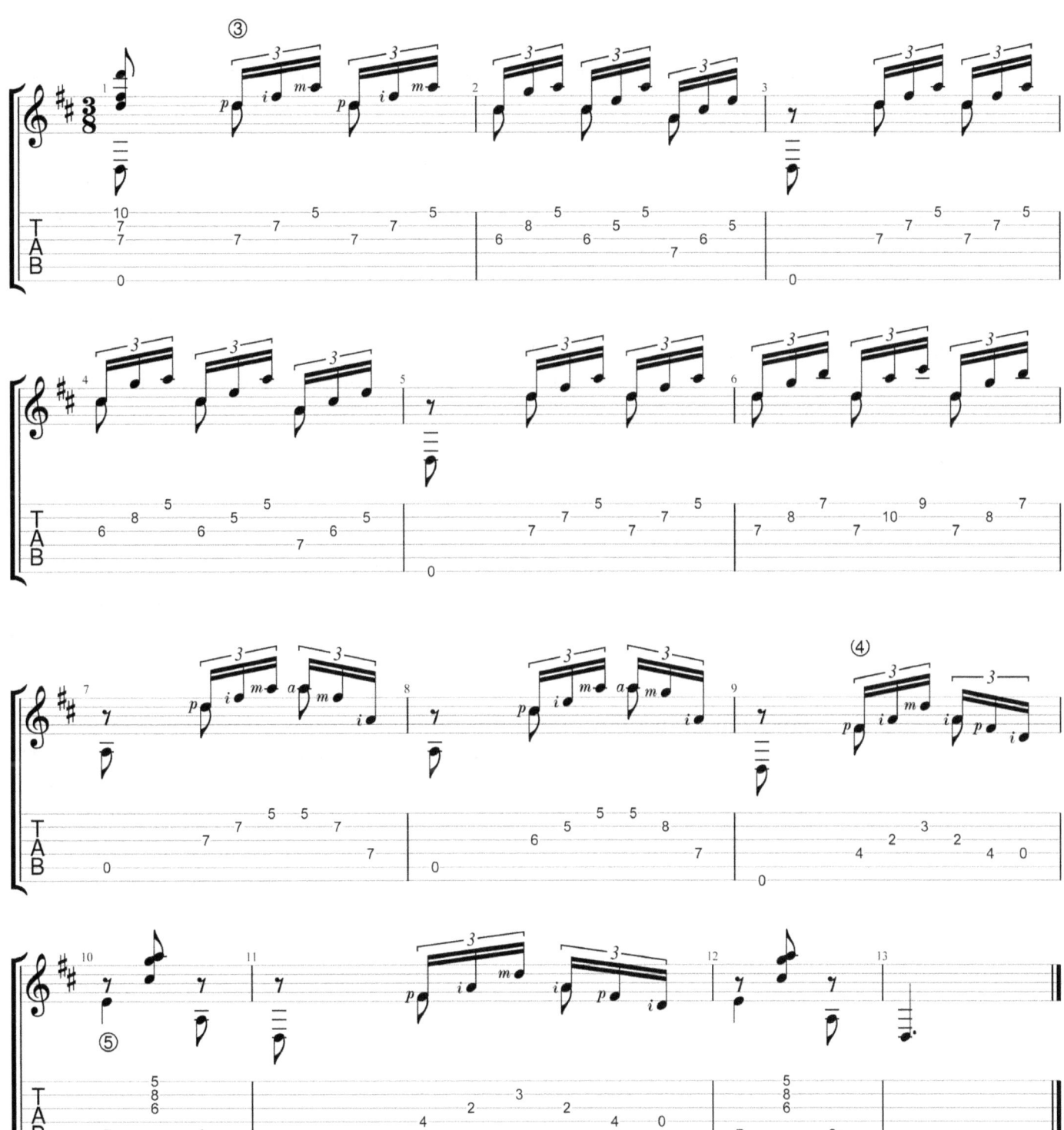

Chapter Seven: Training the Thumb

Basic principles

The thumb is one of the most neglected areas among classical guitarists, yet it is almost impossible to play most intermediate or advanced repertoire without it. When it comes to facilitating the development of the thumb, there are nowhere near the number of specific development exercises as there are for the fingers. Often the thumb is a concessionary addition to finger exercises.

The first two exercises below may look simple in notation but are to be played exclusively with the thumb. This will make them considerably more challenging. Make sure that you keep your thumb joints straight as you play, never curving your thumb inwards. If you have a thumb that naturally bends outwards as you stretch it, that is okay, otherwise you should always keep it straight at all times during playing.

Make sure that your thumb does not move outwards/away from the guitar as you release the string. Keep it as close as you can to the strings following the stroke. This will help you to push the string down as you pluck, imitating the technique employed by the fingers (explained in the tone development chapter) in order to produce a richer sound. For the first two exercises you should use free strokes.

Example 7a

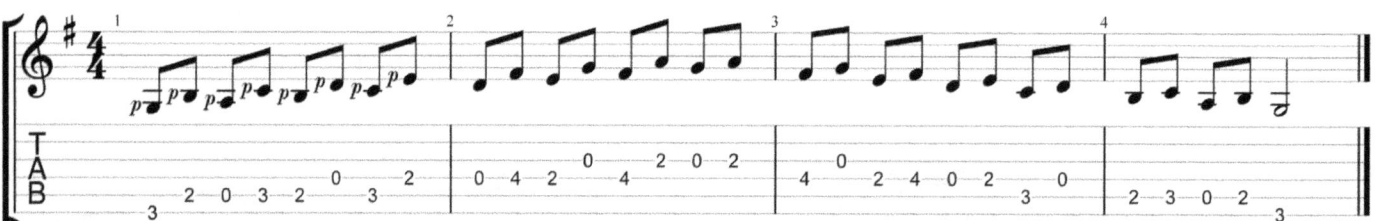

This second exercise is designed to train the ability of the thumb to move between different strings in quick succession. As you play through it, keep monitoring your thumb posture to ensure it does not bend. Keep it straight, but relaxed and loose. Play slowly and, once comfortable, take the exercise to faster tempos. At all times, however, ensure to keep the thumb loose.

Example 7b

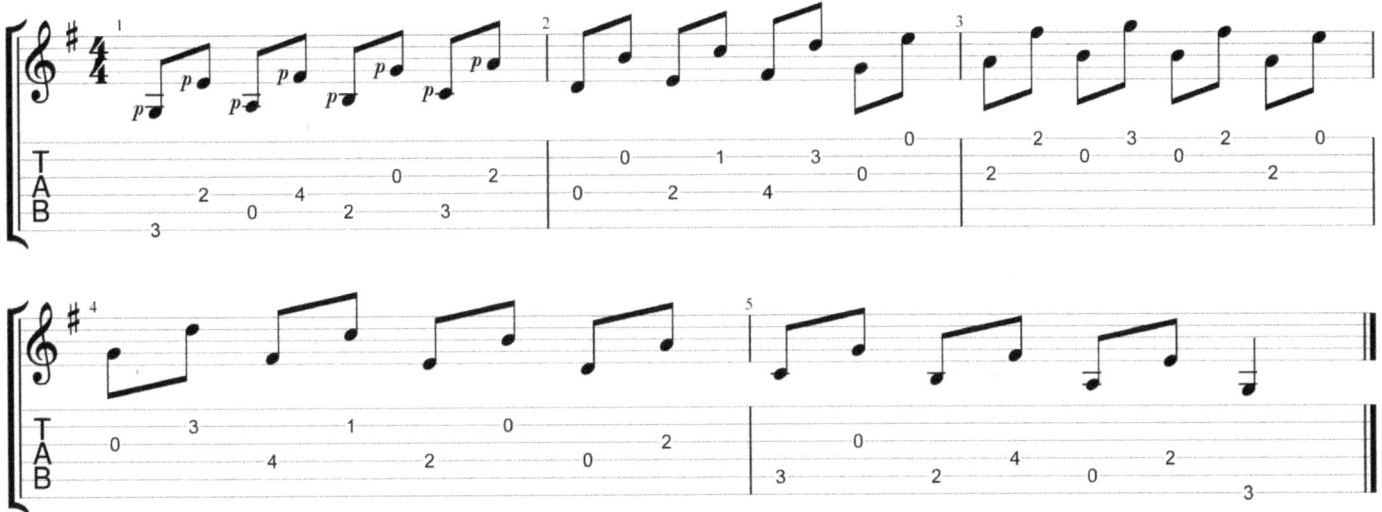

Thumb rest stroke

Amongst thumb techniques, the thumb rest stroke is probably the most neglected of all. The following two scales are designed to be played exclusively with your thumb using rest strokes. Be patient and aim for accuracy. As you work, keep a close eye on your overall hand position, and try to change it as little as possible from its original playing shape. This can be difficult, but is very important, particularly once you move on to the exercises that follow and other aspects of this technique!

Example 7c

Example 7d

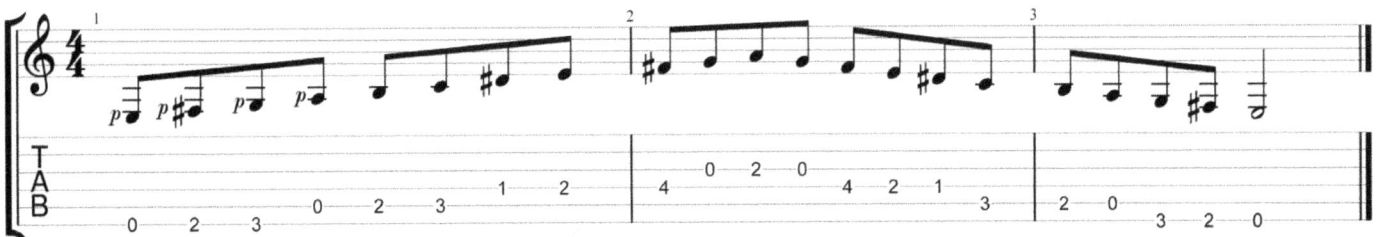

Phrases containing rest strokes with thumb and fingers

Playing rest strokes with the thumb can be challenging, particularly if you are not used to doing it already. However, there is one thing that can make this aspect of technique more challenging still: when you have to follow a thumb rest stroke with a rest stroke played by another finger.

As you will have noticed, your thumb's angle of approach to the string is different when you play rest strokes to when you play free strokes. There is a good chance that, in order to easily *rest* against the adjacent string after picking, your thumb is moving towards the upper plate of the guitar as it moves towards the pluck. This helps to achieve a good rest stroke. However, it can also result in a significant change to the position of your hand. This can prove problematic if the stroke needs to be followed by another rest stoke with one of the other fingers.

In order to counter this, ensure that the angle of approach of your thumb is such that it allows for a good rest stroke, while minimising its effect on the overall position of your hand. Your other fingers must still be well positioned to execute good rest strokes. This is easier said than done and it will take time to condition your hand to naturally approach things in this way. Use the following three exercises to help train your thumb and fingers to do this.

Keep an eye on your wrist. If your hand position changes considerably when playing thumb rest strokes, you will start to see that it tends to bend outwards. This should, of course, be avoided.

Example 7e

Example 7f

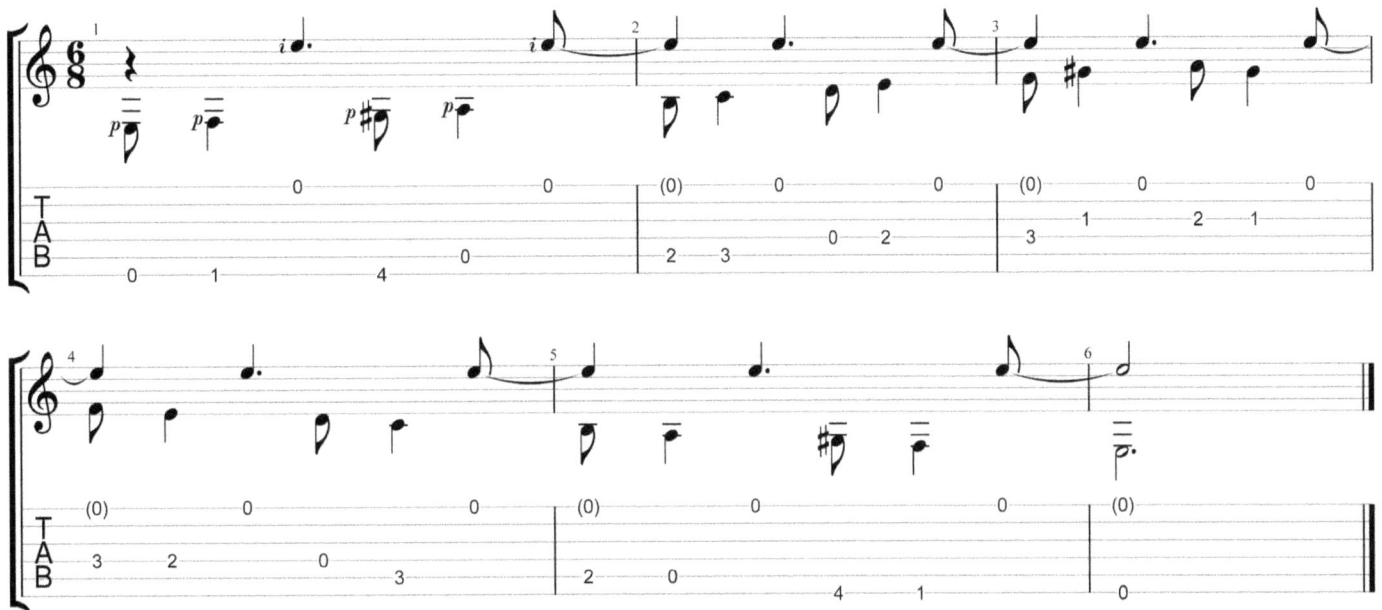

The following exercise alternates every note between thumb (p) and index (i). This approach to moving melodies is very common, particularly in Spanish and Latin American classical guitar repertoire, as well as Flamenco. As with the previous exercises, it is a way of giving the low end of the instrument the lead melodic role and providing simple accompaniment with the upper register (the repetitive open high E note).

This kind of phrase is most commonly played with free strokes, but serves as a great way to test your ability to play alternating rest strokes between the thumb and the fingers. Once you do this, use the same exercise to apply different combinations of rest strokes and free strokes (thumb rest strokes with finger free strokes, thumb free strokes with finger rest strokes).

Example 7g

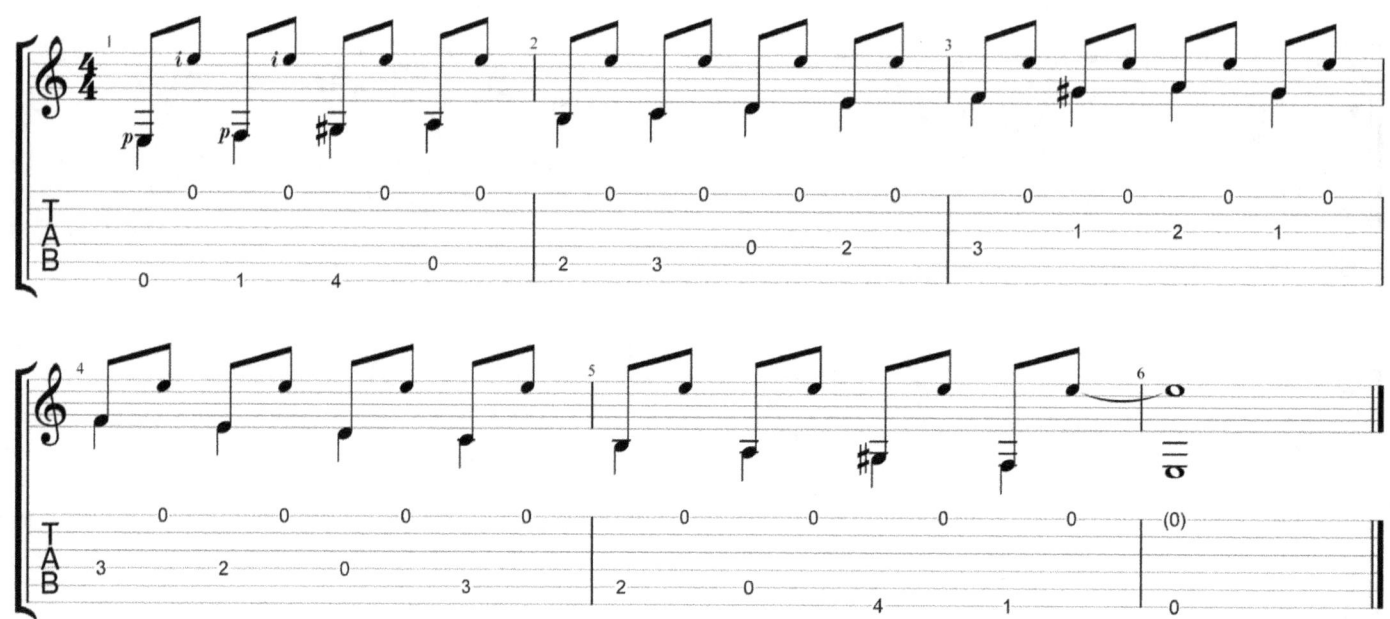

Thumb string alternation and arpeggios

Below are a series of finger combinations inspired by blues and bluegrass music. Although they are not a regular feature of traditional classical repertoire, they do serve as a great complimentary training routine to stimulate the quick response of the thumb, as well as its combination with intricate arpeggio picking patterns.

Example 7h

Example 7i

Example 7j

Example 7k

Chapter Eight: Finger-Thumb Alternation and Tremolo

Achieving sustain on the guitar

As with any other instrument, the classical guitar has its strengths and weaknesses in terms of the possibilities for sound production it offers the player. So far, we have discussed a number of these. In this chapter we will focus on one of the most well-known and extensively used techniques on the instrument, which originated in order to counter one of the disadvantages.

As you will recall from the legato chapter, the loudest moment of any note you play occurs immediately after you pluck it. After the initial attack, the string vibrates less and less until it stops altogether. Therefore, in order to create sustain, players repeatedly pick the same string/note for the sound to continue. This technique is called *tremolo*. It is most often used in between playing other notes in a passage. It can be a challenging technique and has a number of principles which should be studied carefully.

The most important thing to remember when working on these exercises is to aim for an *even* sound and spacing between the notes. Only this will create the effective *illusion* of sustain. To begin, you will play one of the most popular passages of the Spanish guitar repertoire – a section from the flamenco piece *Malagueña*.

Keep all of your fretting hand fingers on each note for as long as possible, until they are forced to move to the next one. With your picking hand, aim for a quick stroke (not a fast tempo of playing), to reduce the time the fingers are in contact with the string and the noise this inevitably produces.

Example 8a

Play the exercise above with each of the following picking hand patterns until you can play them with ease at a medium-fast tempo. Remember, this is all about achieving an *evenness* of sound and timing between the notes. Work on this and make it an integral part of your daily practice routine for about a month or more.

p, m, p, m, p, m, etc

p, a, p, a, p, a, etc

p, i, p, m, p, i, etc

p, m, p, i, p, m, etc

p, i, p, a, p, i, etc

p, a, p, i, p, a, etc

p, m, p, a, p, m, etc

p, a, p, m, p, a, etc

Two-note tremolo

For added intensity and flair, many pieces incorporate more than one repetition of the *sustained* note in-between other notes in the part. This is a very important aspect of the technique and one of the best technical development exercises for the picking hand in general. It demands a great amount of response and coordination. As always, it is the *evenness* that makes it!

Keeping the hand in place

It is absolutely key whenever working on a tremolo pattern that the hand stays in place. As the fingers work on their intricate patterns, ensure that the posture of the hand is not affected to any great extent. Very often, particularly when a player is new to this technique, the hand will tend to bounce up and down a bit, which causes it to move from its natural playing position. Remember, the fingers are doing the main work, not the arm, nor palm of your hand. Keep an eye on your wrist and keep it as still and relaxed as possible.

Example 8b

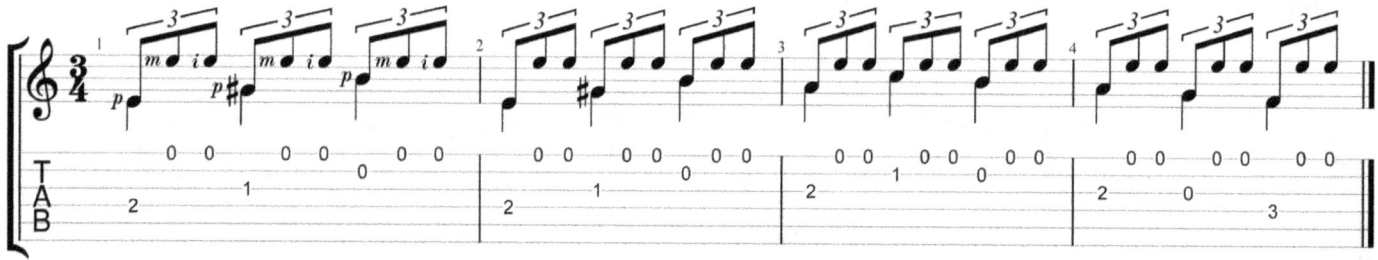

Next, you will develop the ability to use all fingers to play such patterns. Although it can be repetitive, the looseness and response that comes from mastering the exercise above with each of the following finger patterns is so worth the patience! Remember, you are supposed to develop this skill over time; you don't have to spend hours only working on this every day. It should be one component of a much larger list of things to work on.

Repeat the above exercise with the following picking hand finger patterns for five to ten minutes a day. Do this for as long as needed until they feel, and sound, completely comfortable. You should only be working on one of these at a time until mastered, before moving on to the next.

p, m, i, p, m, i, etc

p, i, m, p, i, m, etc

p, a, i, p, a, i, etc

p, i, a, p, i, a, etc

p, a, m, p, a, m, etc

p, m, a, p, m, a, etc

Three-note tremolo

As you might expect, the two-note tremolo naturally progresses to the three-note tremolo. This is by far the most difficult of the three to play evenly, as the cycle of movement of the fingers is much longer. As before, work gradually to master all the different fingering combinations suggested. Master each one before moving on to the next.

Example 8c

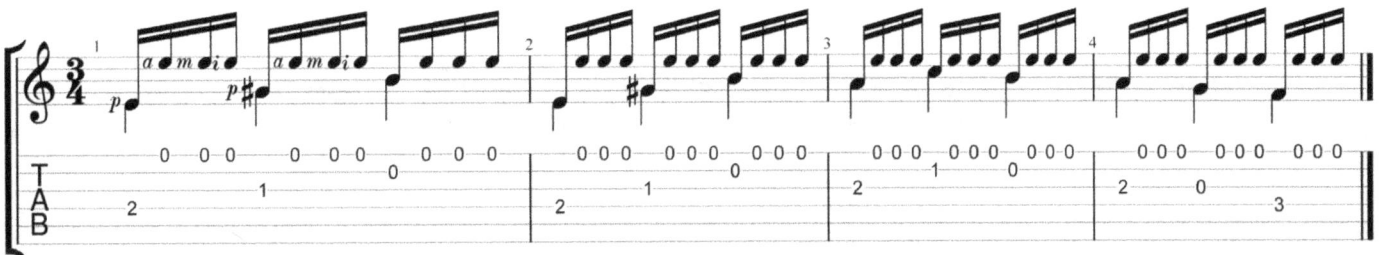

p, i, m, a, p, i, m, a, etc

p, m, i, a, p, m, i, a, etc

p, m, a, i, p, m, a, i, etc

p, i, a, m, p, i, a, m, etc

p, a, i, m, p, a, i, m, etc

Strengthening each stroke

An effective way to improve the fingers' performance when playing *tremolo* is to put an accent on a note (or number of notes) within a pattern. This way, each finger is required to work on its volume and presence individually. It is also a great test of how well each finger responds to your brain's orders!

Try the following exercises:

Example 8d

Example 8e

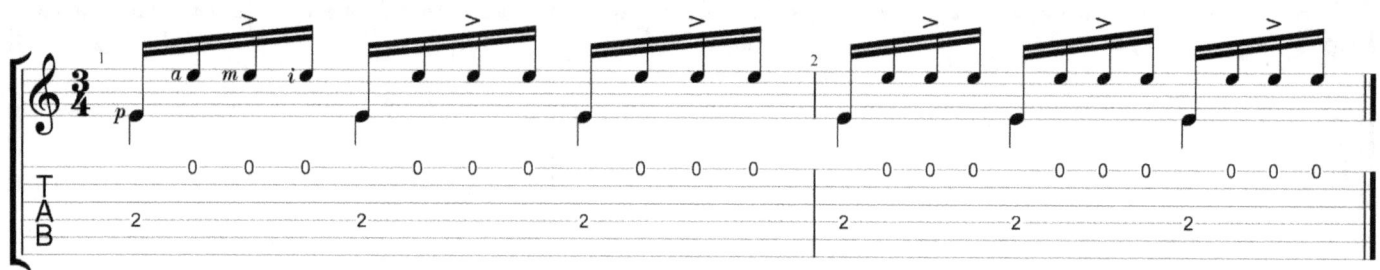

Example 8f

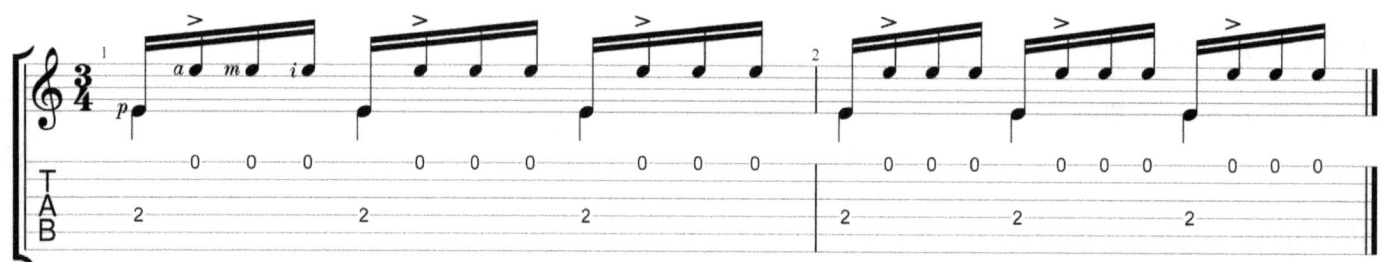

Example 8g

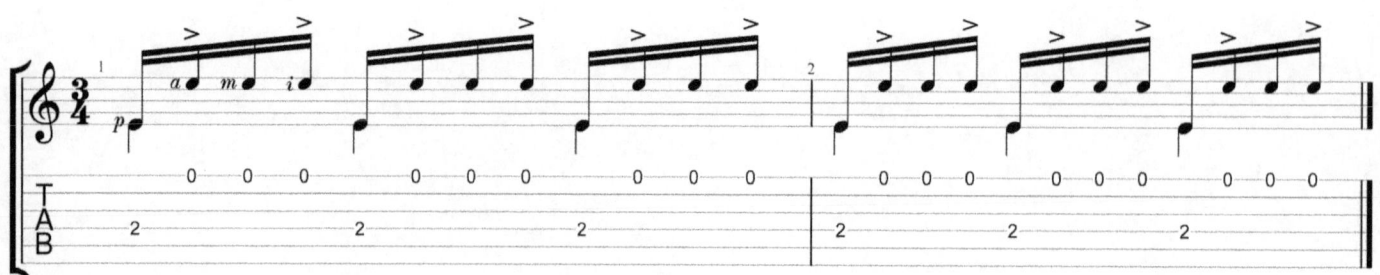

Example 8h

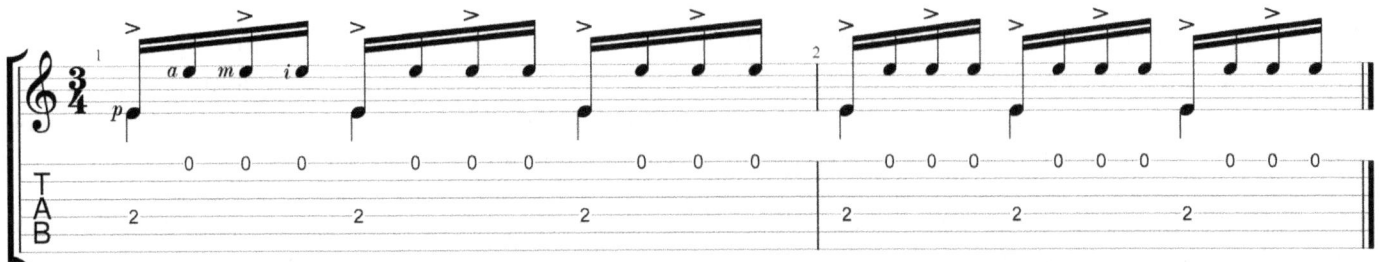

Chapter Nine: Refining Scales and Single-Line Melodic Playing

The classical guitar is mostly played as a solo instrument. Given its ability to play harmony, melody and rhythm, all on one instrument, composers have made it a priority to maximise this potential more than writing for the guitar as a purely melodic or harmonic/accompanying instrument. This, interestingly, is often the opposite way around in many other genres of music that use the guitar.

Nevertheless, playing single-note melodies is still an important aspect of classical guitar language. There are pieces where the guitar plays a melodic role exclusively, as well as passages within solo repertoire where there is only one melodic line.

Non-arpeggiated

It is worth mentioning that, for the purpose of this section of the book we are not referring to *arpeggiated* melodies. In that scenario the notes are played one at a time, but left to ring, creating a sense of harmony. Here I am referring to melodies where each note stops before a new one is played. Such melodic construction is often, though not only, based on scales more than arpeggios.

Rest stroke

For this section of the book you will work on the ability of your picking hand fingers to play *rest strokes*. As you may remember, a rest stroke is achieved by the finger plucking the string, then following straight through to rest onto the adjacent string.

Remember that the movement of the picking finger should always originate from the knuckle of the hand, as opposed to the smaller joints on the length of your finger. This ensures you use the full strength of the finger, producing a bigger sound with less effort, and avoiding tension and fatigue.

Scale practice

There are different schools of thought when it comes to playing scales on the guitar. Some players have more experience playing position scales (one or two octave patterns which are mostly located in a single position). Many classical players, however, are very good at playing scales which constantly move in and out of different positions, using the length of the neck.

The best players will feel comfortable doing both, and understand the scale not only as an exercise, but as a sequence of specific intervals which they can relocate to different parts of the fretboard. That said, scales are a fantastic way to develop technical ability, accuracy, coordination and speed.

There are many learning resources dedicated exclusively to playing scales. Here, I am going to give you patterns that are useful for playing essential scales in ways you can easily transpose to different keys. All the scale patterns that follow are moveable. You will be able to learn *in-position* and *between-positions* patterns for each of them. Learn each one, then move it to different keys by playing the same pattern starting from another note on the same string. If you run out of fretboard, just play the scale as far as the guitar allows you to.

Each of the scales below should be played with the following picking approaches:

- *i, m, i, m,* etc
- *m, i, m, i,* etc
- With a continuous use of the thumb (*p*) for all notes on the lower three strings of the guitar (4: D, 5: A and 6: low E), followed by each of the previous two patterns on the upper three strings (1: high E, 2: B and 3: G).

Keep in mind that some of the scale patterns are better suited for use in repertoire than others, which may be less practical. However, they are all effective for technical practice and as position-shifting exercises. (An example of this is Example 9g below, where the shape moves towards one end of the fretboard before moving towards the other).

C major scale

Example 9a

C major scale

Example 9b

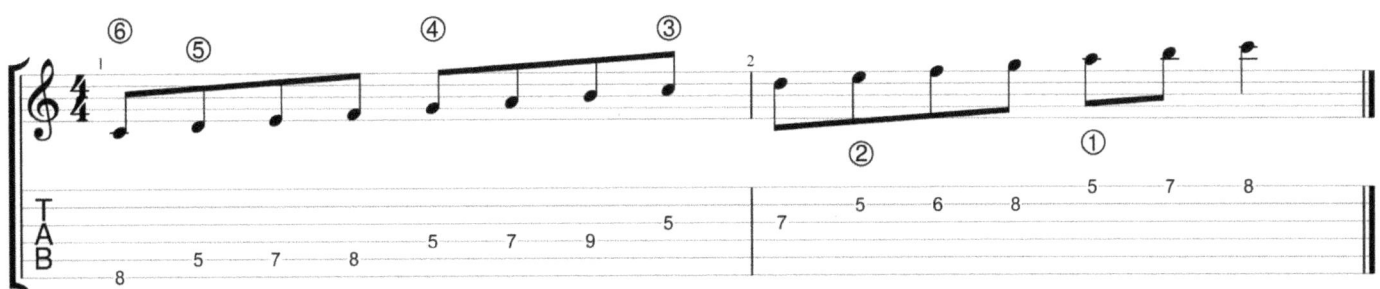

C major scale
Example 9c

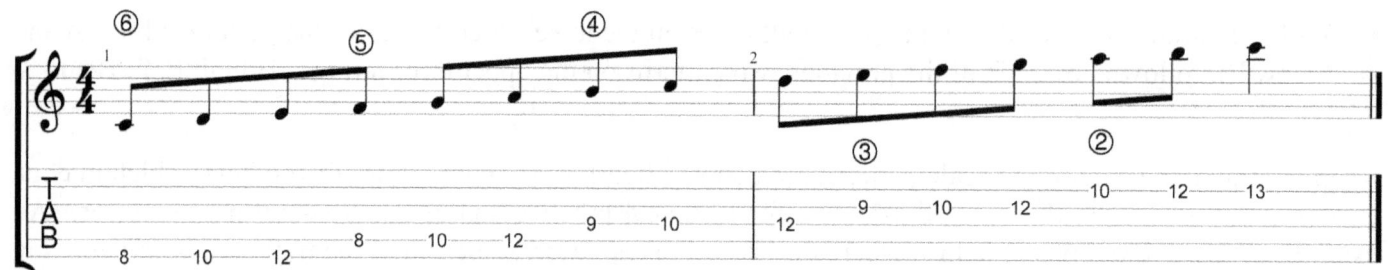

C major scale
Example 9d

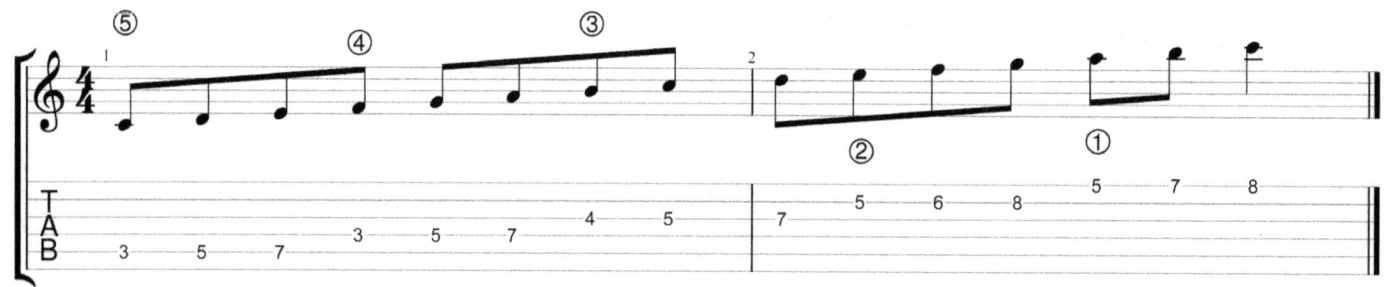

C major scale
Example 9e

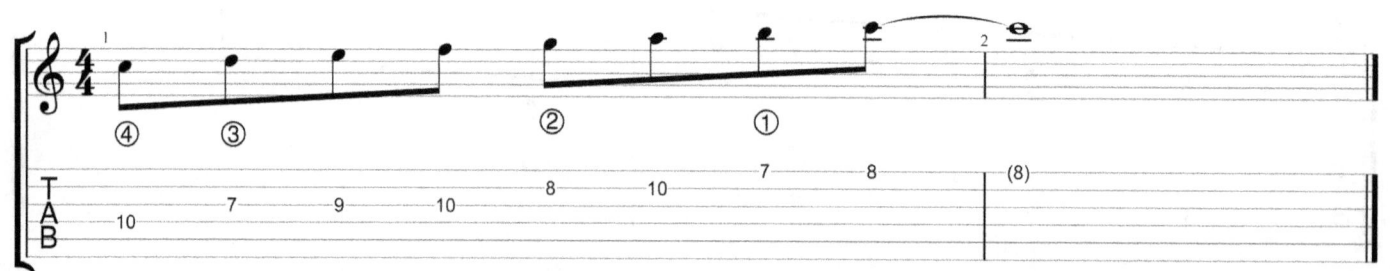

C major scale

Example 9f

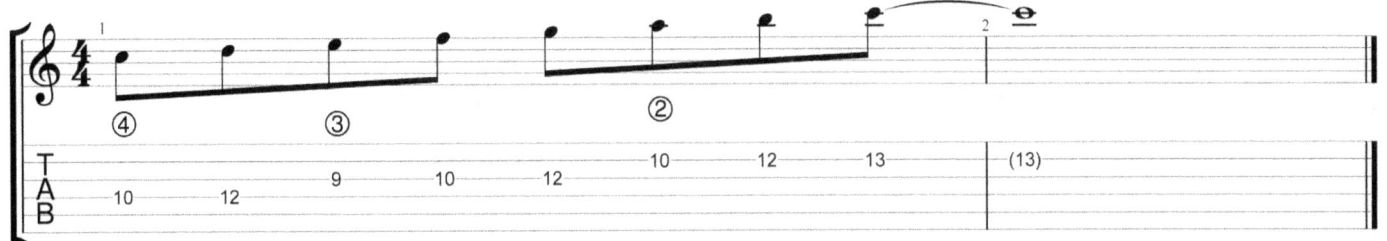

C major scale

Example 9g

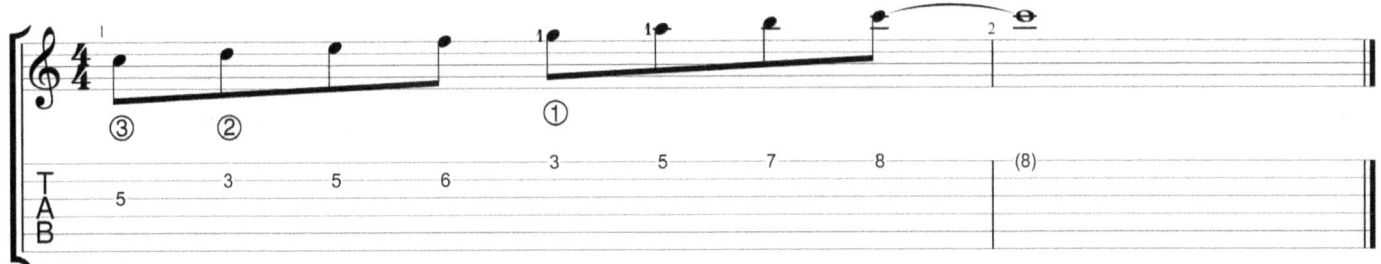

C major scale

Example 9h

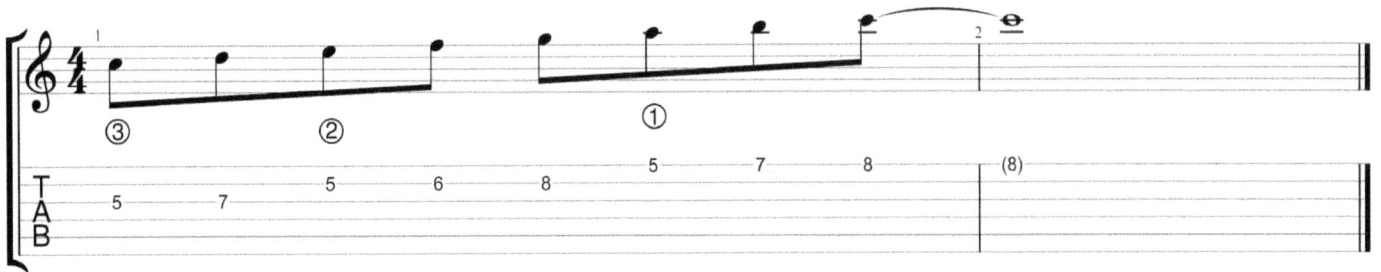

C harmonic minor scale

Example 9i

C harmonic minor scale

Example 9j

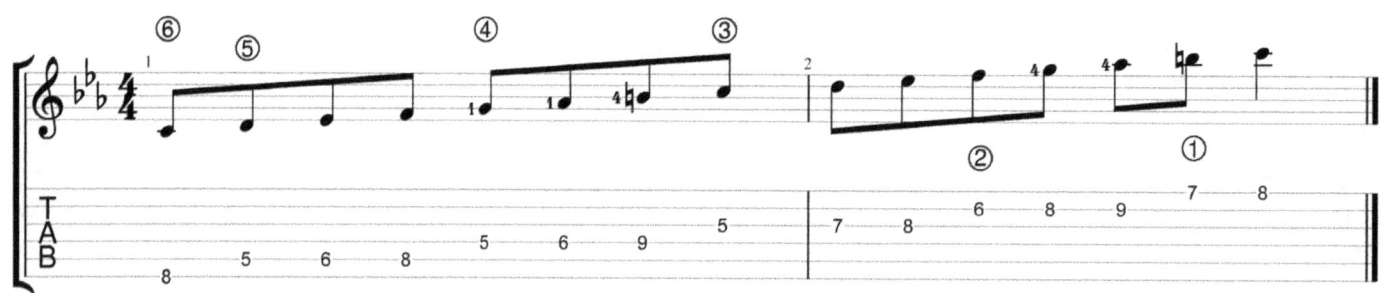

C harmonic minor scale

Example 9k

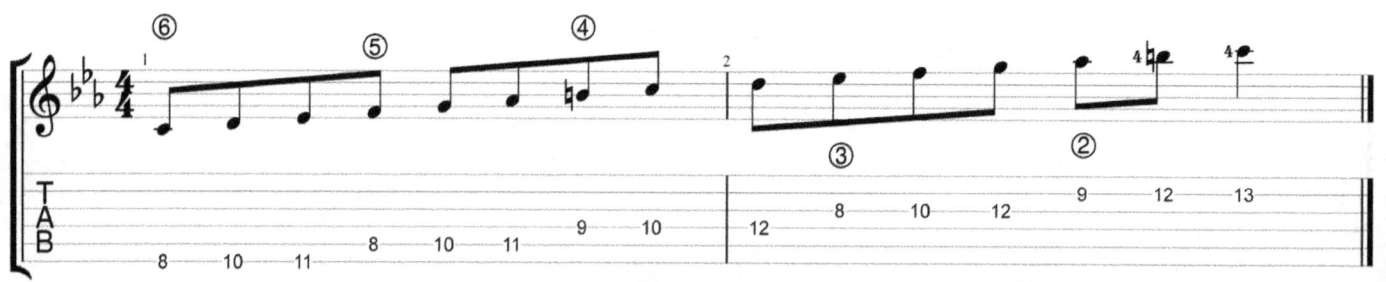

C harmonic minor scale

Example 9l

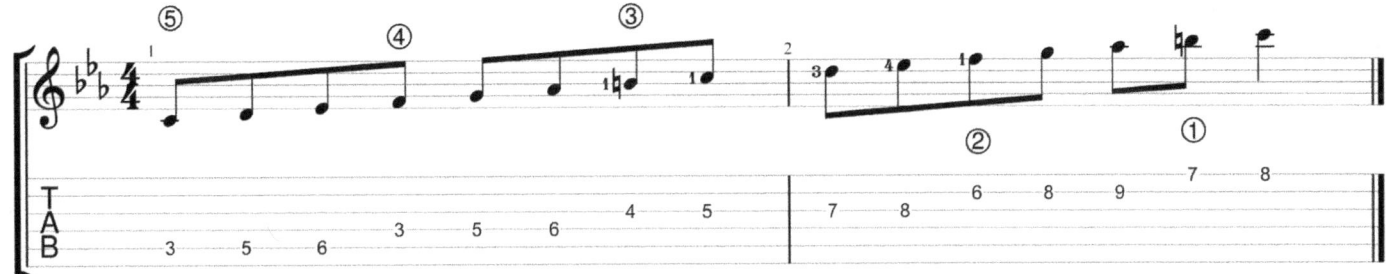

C harmonic minor scale

Example 9m

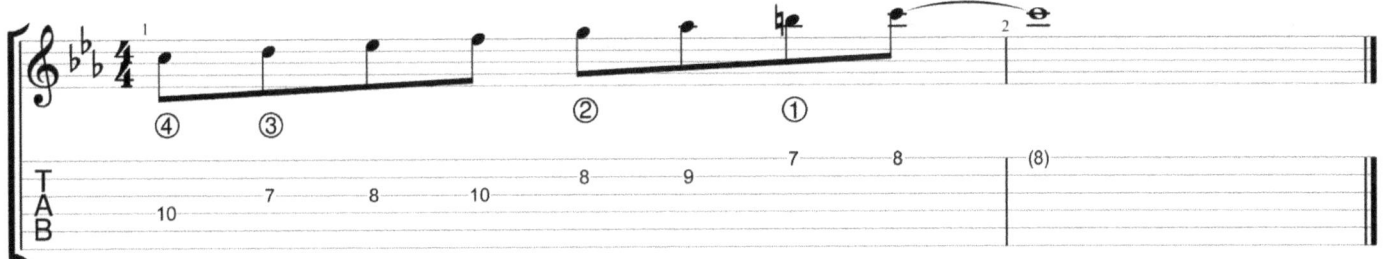

C harmonic minor scale

Example 9n

C harmonic minor scale

Example 9o

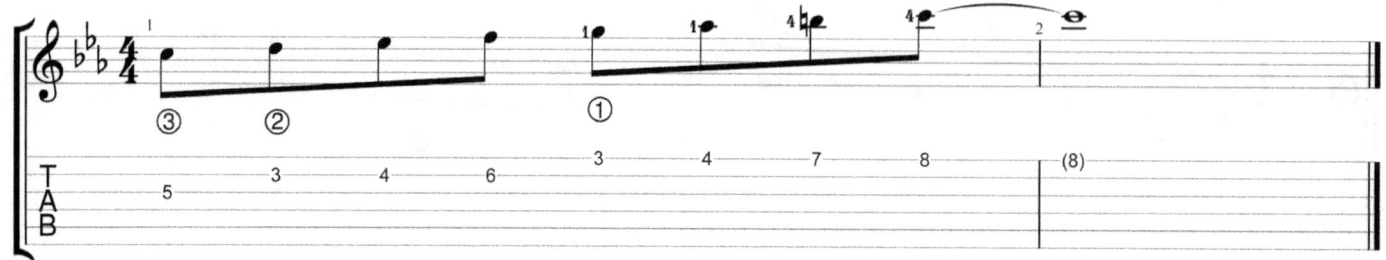

C harmonic minor scale

Example 9p

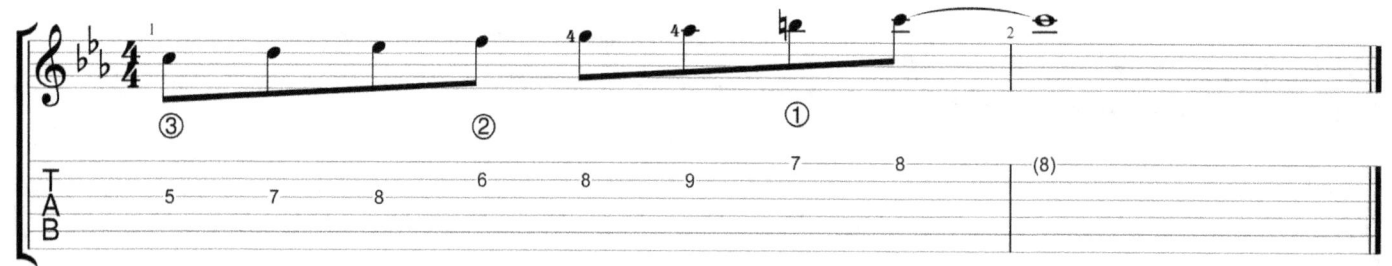

C melodic minor scale scale

Example 9q

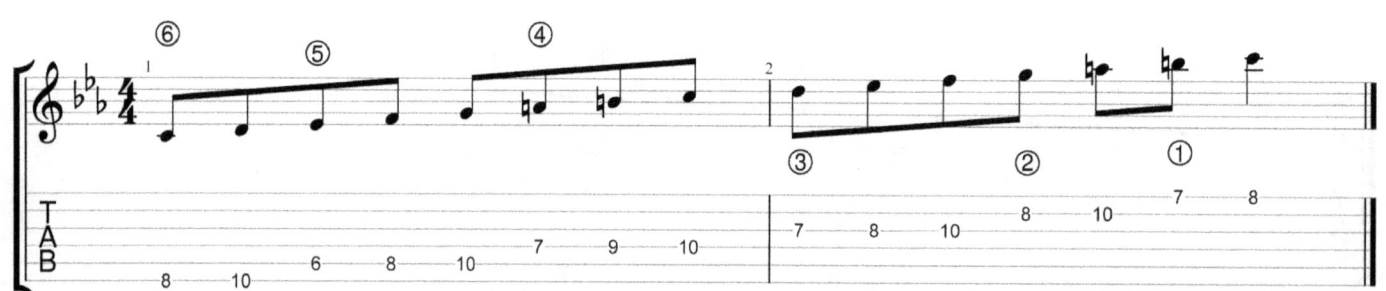

C melodic minor scale
Example 9r

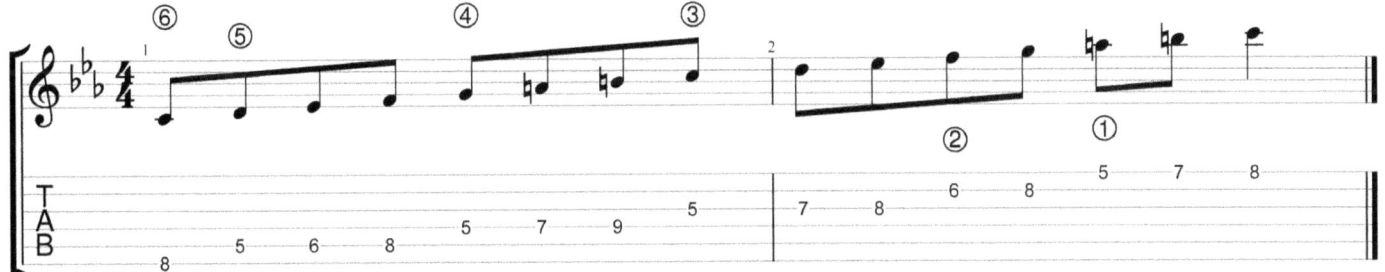

C melodic minor scale
Example 9s

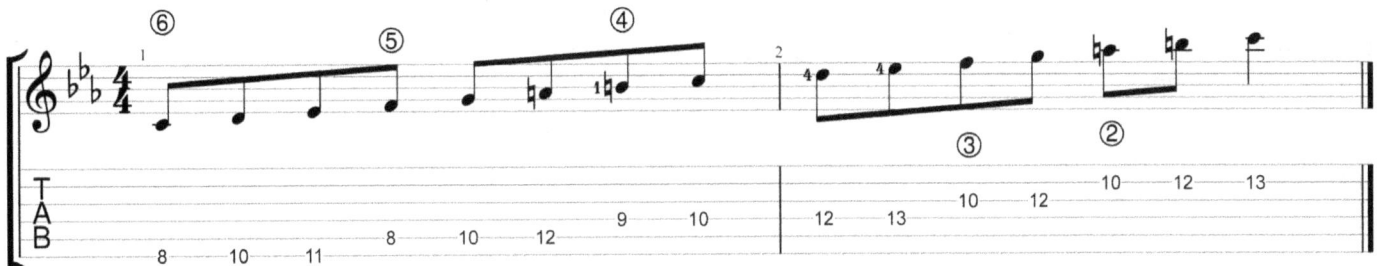

C melodic minor scale
Example 9t

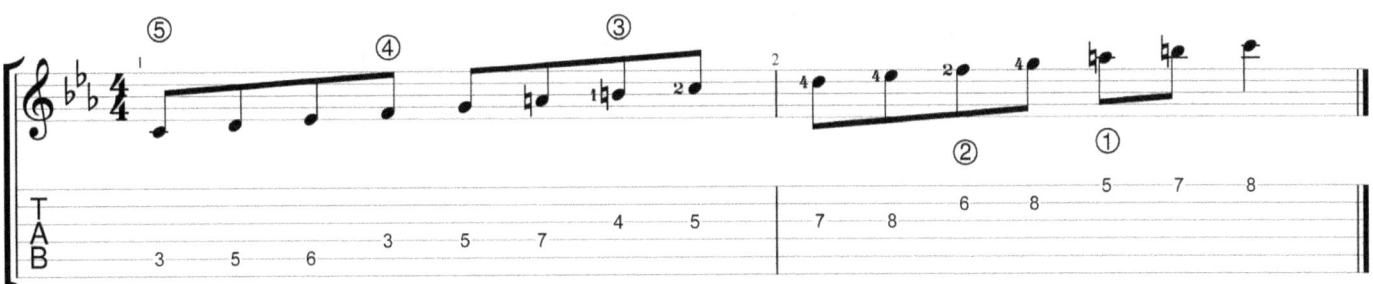

C melodic minor scale

Example 9u

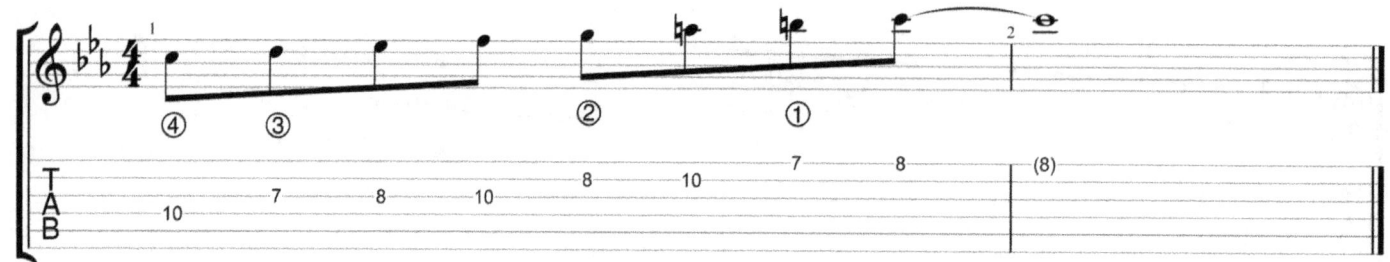

C melodic minor scale

Example 9v

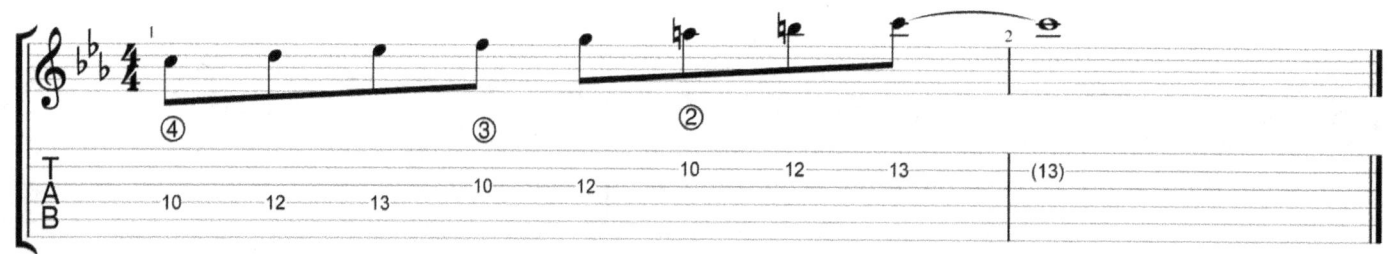

C melodic minor scale

Example 9w

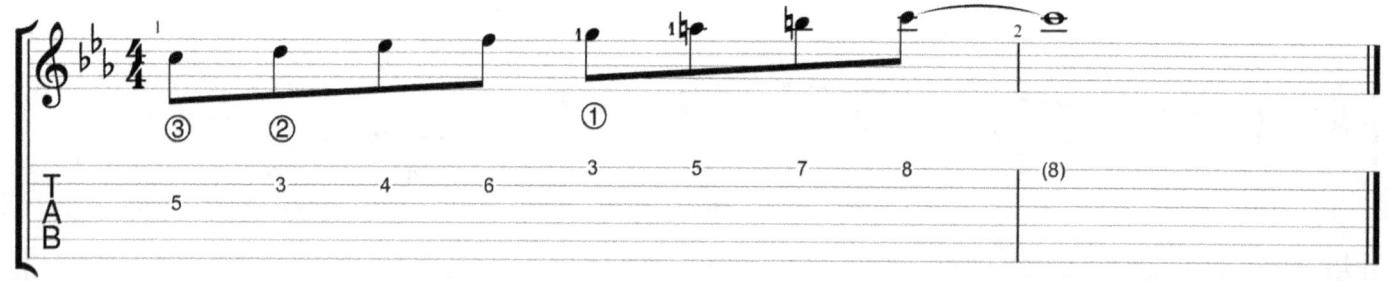

C melodic minor scale

Example 9x

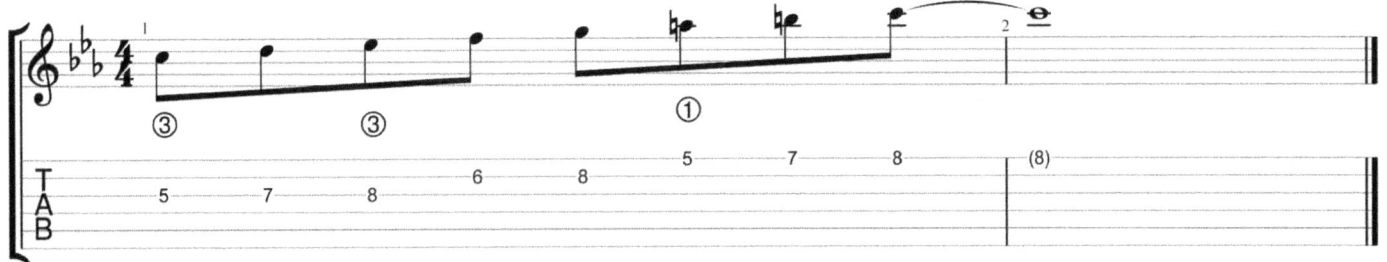

Chapter Ten: Fretboard-Long Repositioned Scale Shapes

Following on from your previous study of scales, you will now play scale shapes that rapidly move up the fretboard, by playing four-note-per-string patterns. This can be disorientating at first, because the fretting hand has to constantly relocate to a new position. Don't play any unnecessary stretches. Follow the fingering suggestions closely, and don't press the notes too hard! Remember the work you did in previous chapters: only apply the force necessary to sound the notes clearly. Forgetting to do this will cause resistance and prevent the fretting hand from moving smoothly across the fretboard.

F major scale

Example 10a

Bb major scale

Example 10b

F harmonic minor scale

Example 10c

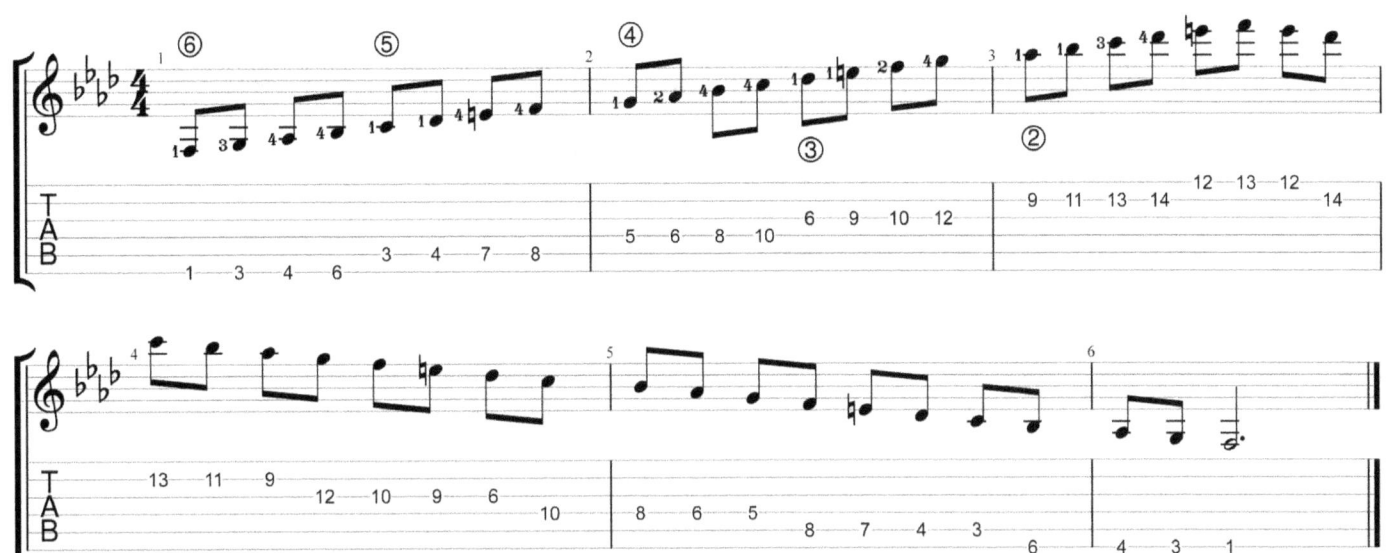

Bb harmonic minor scale

Example 10d

F melodic minor scale

Example 10e

Bb melodic minor scale

Example 10f

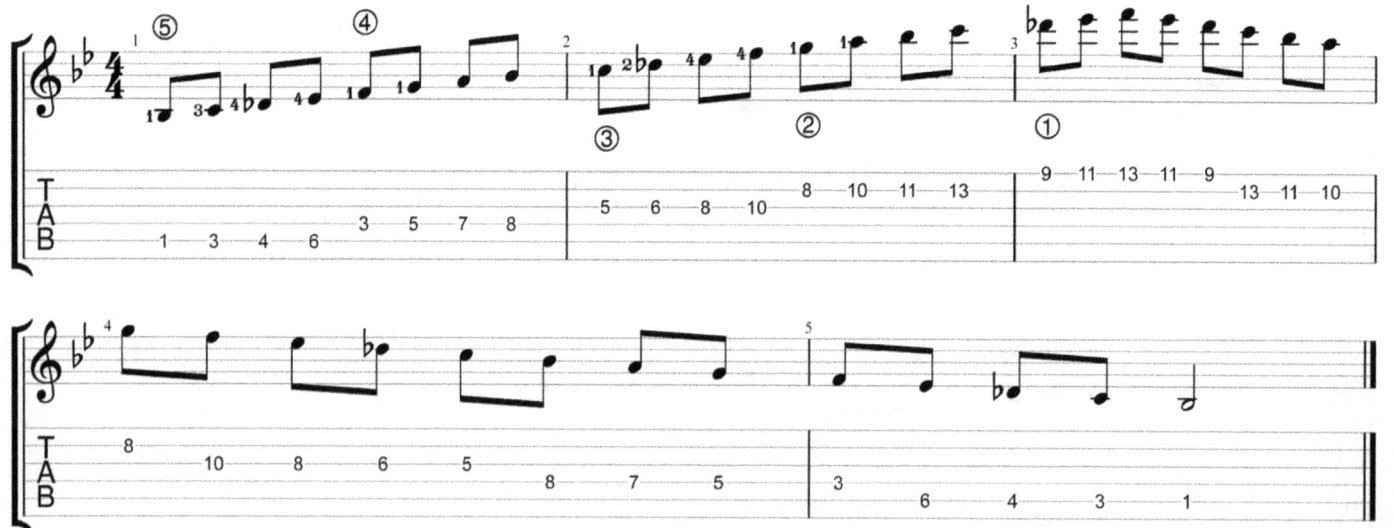

Chapter Eleven: Speed and Dexterity for Rest Strokes

This chapter is an extension of the previous scale chapters and focuses specifically on the development of speed when playing scale-based, single-note melodic lines. It will also develop the ability of the picking fingers to play less conventional patterns and phrases, which can prove challenging when using rest strokes.

Developing speed in melodic playing

It is not rare to find fast single-line melodic passages in advanced classical guitar repertoire. Most frequently, however, a fast passage will appear in the middle of a phrase using a variety of different note values. With this in mind, it is more useful to learn to change speed and play fast, shorter passages, than to play fast for long periods of time. Changing speed can be challenging in itself and requires great finger control.

Of course, it is a good skill to be able to play fast for longer periods, but this can be cultivated gradually as your stamina builds, once short fast phrases have been mastered.

Finger preparation

As with most things on the guitar, it is important to examine everything else that is happening around the strings, other than the picking itself. Controlling these aspects to your advantage will provide you with the best chance of producing the best sound.

In the case of developing speed when playing rest strokes, it is vital to monitor the movement of the fingers when they are *not* picking. Playing quick successive notes requires that immediately after playing, each finger re-positions itself onto the next note it will play as soon as possible. This preparation is as important as the speed of attack on the notes. Without a careful study of it, our chances of playing faster phrases effectively are much smaller.

Alternating fingers

When playing fast passages, most players like to alternate two fingers (most frequently *i* and *m*). However, it is good practice and good finger training to alternate between any other combination of two fingers.

When you play the exercises that follow, half of your concentration should be on the movement of the finger that has just played and its quick relocation to the next note; the other half should be on the attack of the notes by each finger. Synchronicity between the two fingers in the roles of *attacking* and *relocating* is a massive part of what produces great melodic playing. As with *tremolo* technique, it is the evenness between the notes that creates the impression of a really powerful sound (even if the speed is not incredibly fast), as opposed to very fast, uneven playing.

Staccato practice technique

Staccato means that the notes should be detached from one another with a sharply marked space in between.

Applied to a single string, this technique is very effective for the purpose of developing fast melodic playing. This is because, in order to sharply stop the note that has just been played, the alternating finger needs to rapidly rest itself on that same string. This forces the finger to concentrate on the *relocating* aspect of the movement.

To begin, play the simple phrases below, alternating *i* and *m* fingers. Concentrate on the following factors as you play:

- Monitor your *relocating* finger as much as your *playing* finger

- Play staccato. As soon as a string is played, sharply stop its sound with the opposite finger by resting it on the string

- The alternation of the fingers should be carefully synchronised. One finger moves in one direction to pluck, while the other moves in the opposite direction in order to relocate. No finger should be resting in one place for a while then moving abruptly. There should be a continuous flow of movement

- As always, play slow and aim for accuracy first. Only once this is achieved, increase the speed gradually

Example 11a

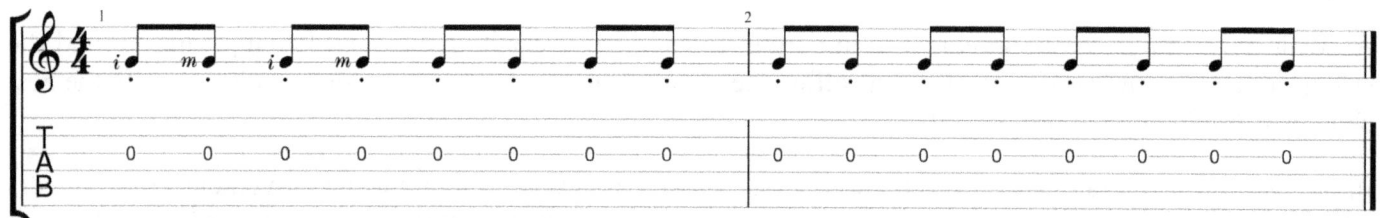

Example 11b

Example 11c

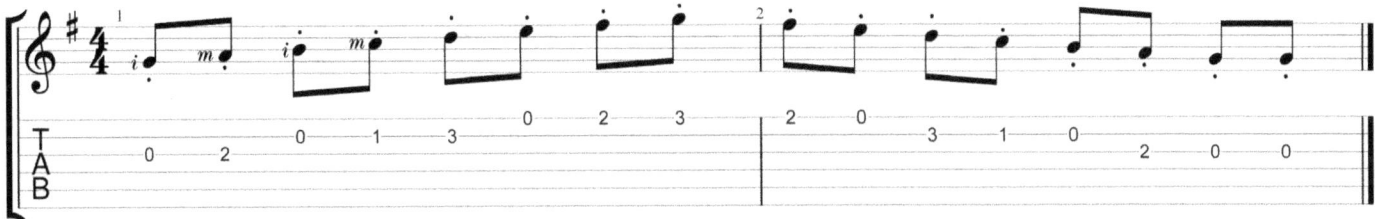

The next exercises introduce changes in speed. This is the type of passage referred to earlier, that often occurs in repertoire. Pay attention to ensure that the transitions between straight quavers, triplets and semiquavers are as precise as possible, without any gradual *slowing down* or *speeding up* from one note value to the next. There should be a smooth transition. Observe the principles mentioned above.

Example 11d

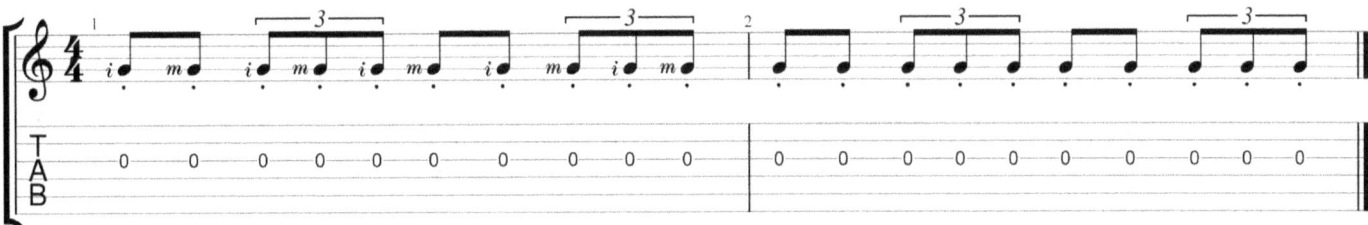

Example 11e

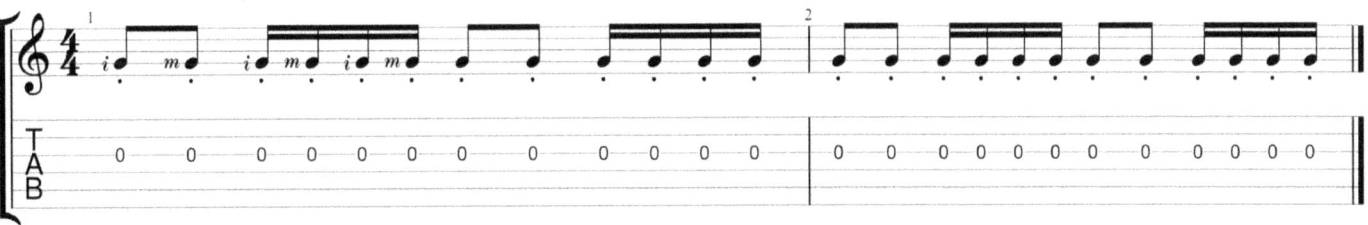

Example 11f

Example 11g

Example 11h

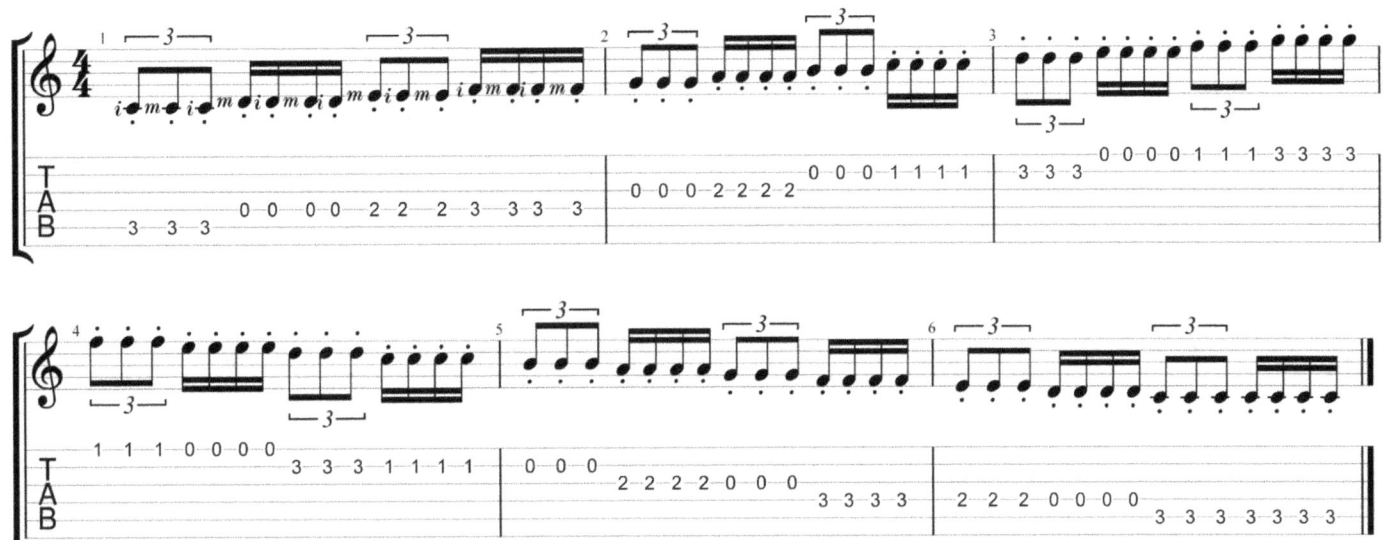

Maintaining speed

The next two exercises do not have a change in speed. They will be your first attempt at maintaining one fast note value running for an extended phrase. I recommend that you work towards playing the examples at 90bpm, which is a good standard for this kind of exercise.

As you become comfortable playing at such tempos, gradually work towards faster ones. Always work with a metronome and increase tempo gradually, between two to four beats per minute faster, never jumping to one that is considerably quicker. This is the best way to condition the hands to be able to do things they couldn't before. You will be able to closely monitor everything your hands are doing, and this will ensure that each new challenge is conquered in a shorter space of time. As a result, you will feel like you are achieving more on a regular basis.

Example 11i

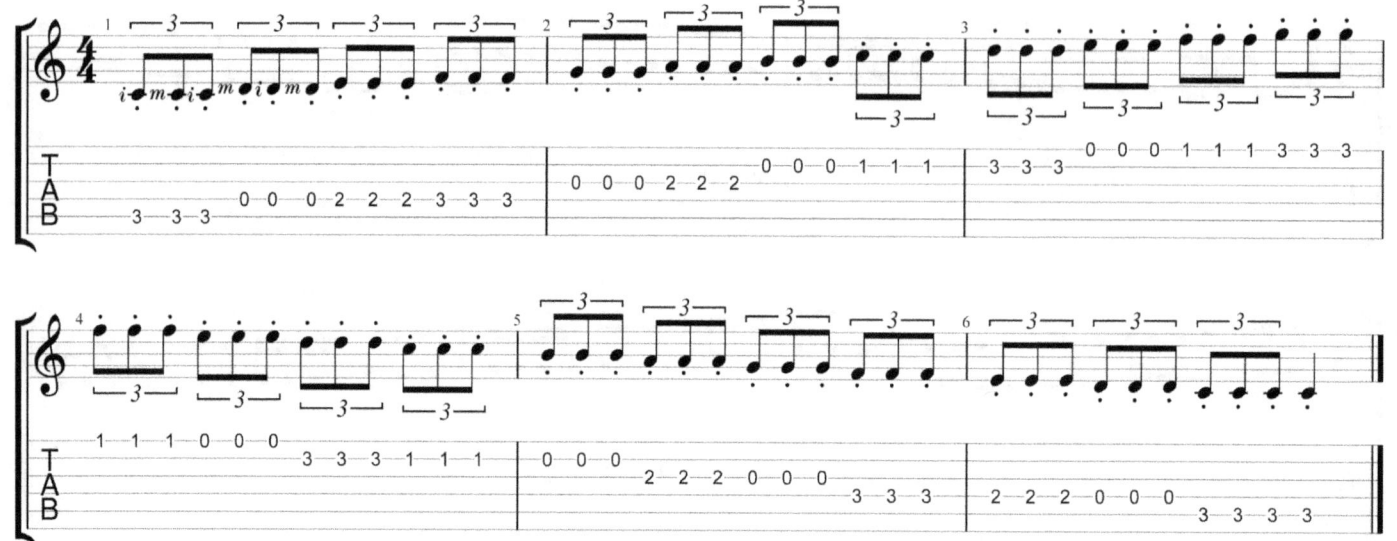

Example 11j

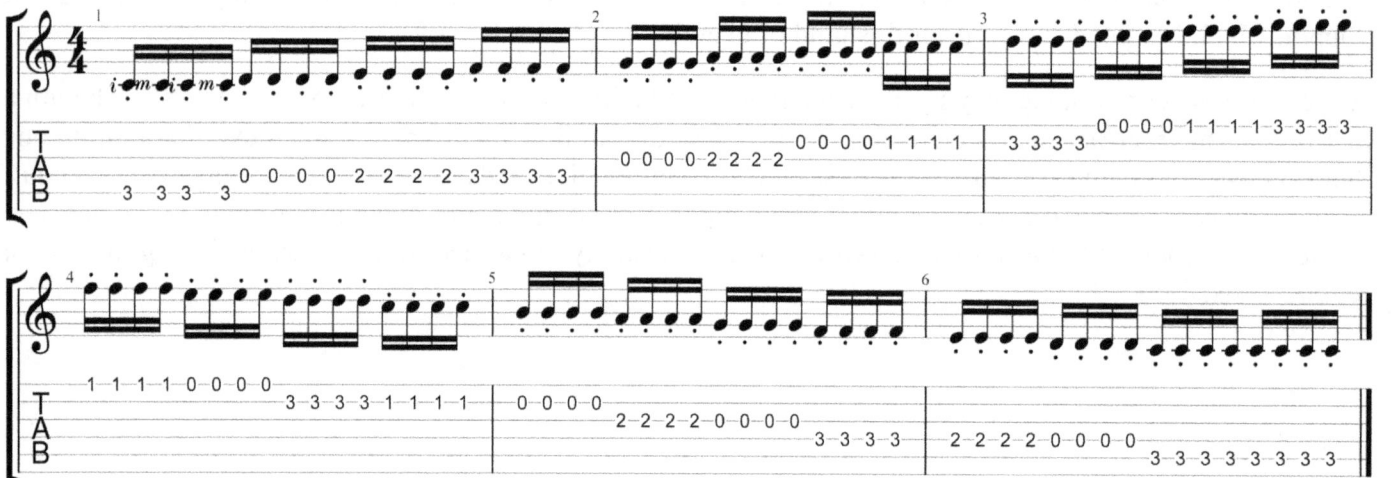

Example 11k

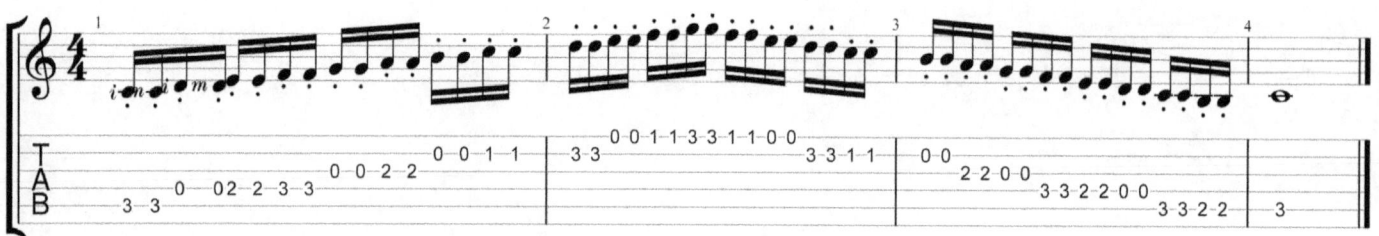

Developing dexterity for challenging melodic shapes with rest strokes

One of the most difficult things to do when playing alternating rest strokes on the classical guitar is to transition from one string to another. This section is dedicated to helping you train your fingers to play such phrases with more ease. Don't worry about applying *staccato* technique, as it is impractical when moving between strings.

Each of the principles explained so far in this chapter should be used and monitored closely as you continue with the following routines. It is only by continuing to force ourselves to use these principles that, over time, they become our new *natural* way of playing.

Example 111

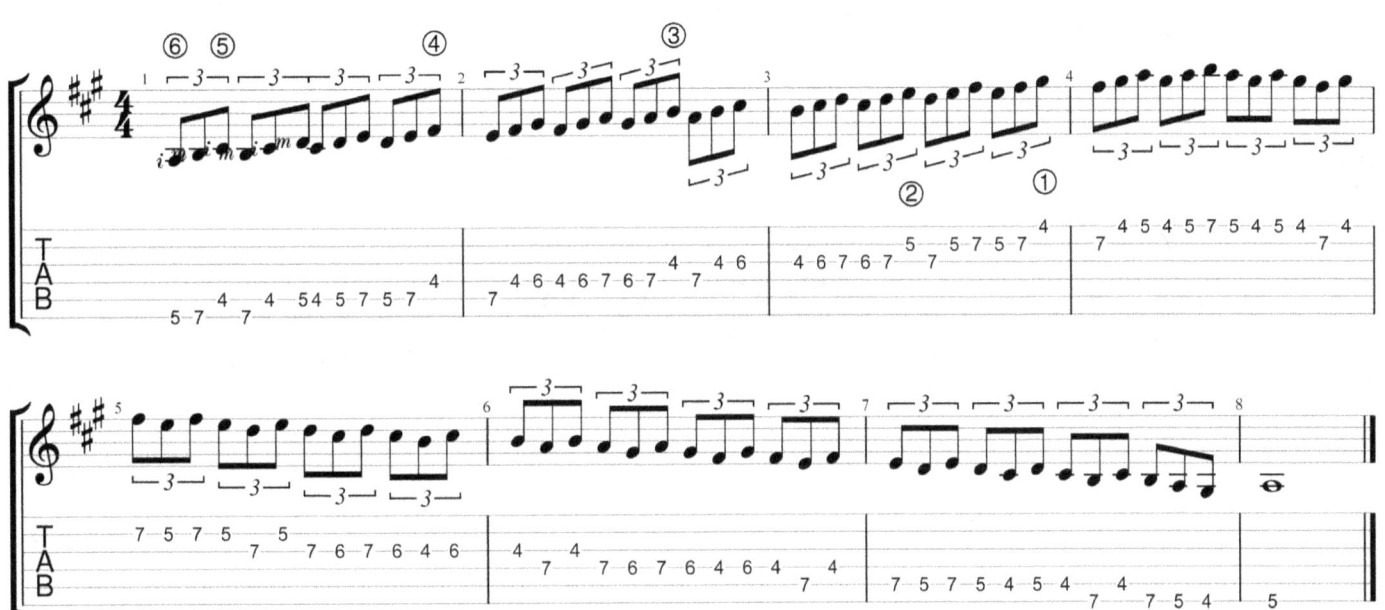

Example 11m

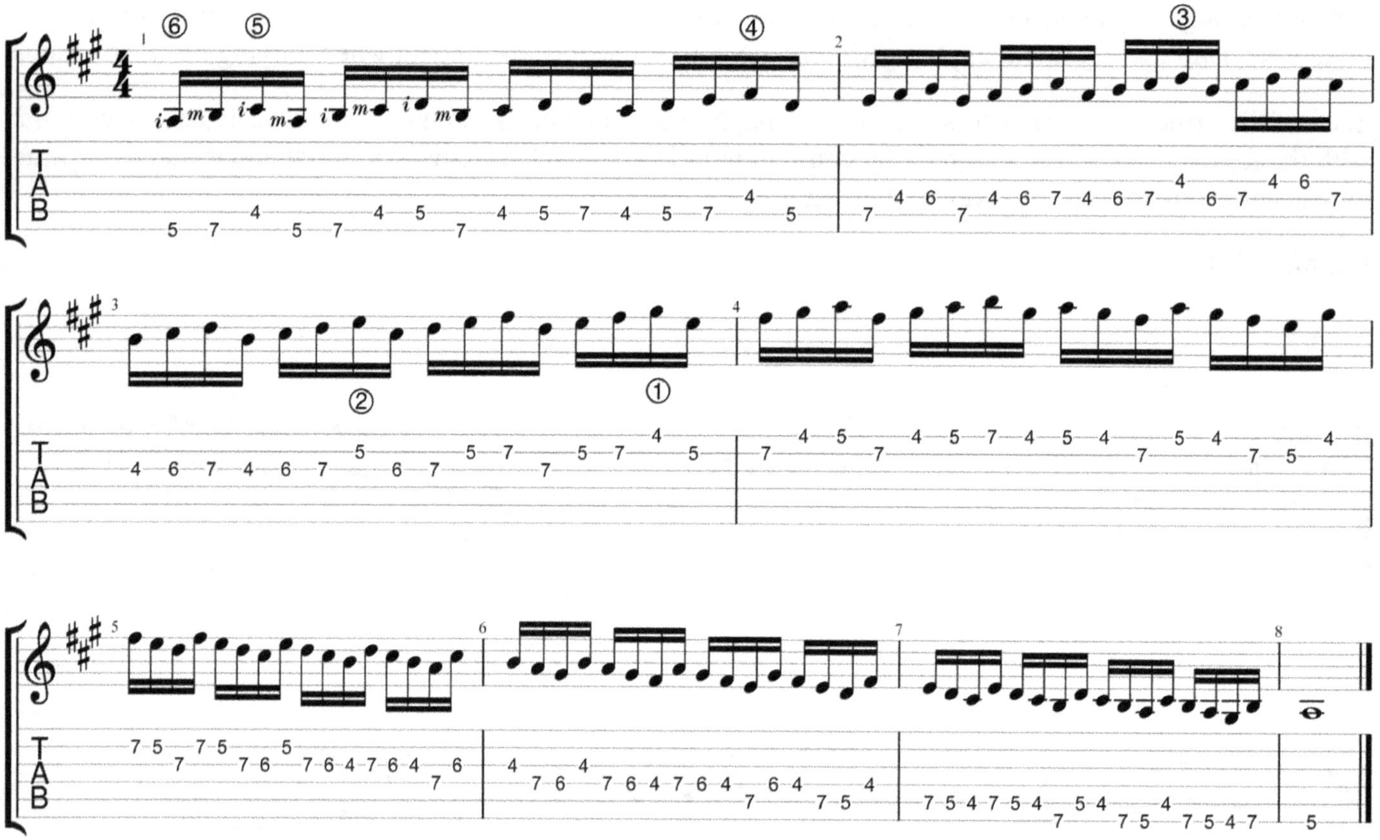

Example 11n

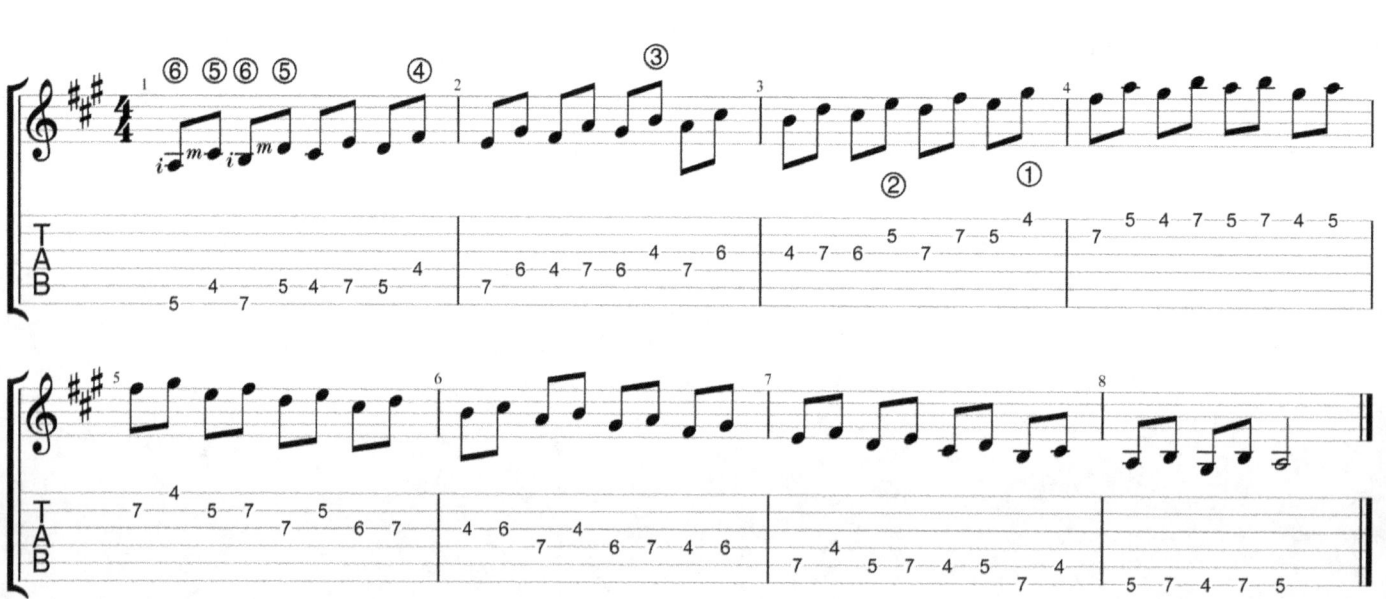

The final example incorporates big intervals. When the intervals are this wide, it is common to alternate between the thumb (*p*) playing the lower notes, and the index finger (*i*) playing the upper notes. For the purpose of this exercise I want you to play it two ways. As I've just described (which will allow you to work on your traditional technique), and also alternating the *i* and *m* fingers (which helps with the coordination of alternating fingers while changing strings).

Example 11o

Chapter Twelve: Rasgueado

Flamenco music and its influence on the classical guitar

Rasgueado comes from flamenco music. It is the term used to refer to the effect of strumming the strings with the nails, usually in a pattern, with a good amount of force and great coordination. Many people, including guitarists, are not aware that the classical and flamenco styles of guitar playing are very different. The fact that they both sound "Spanish" can be misleading. In reality, these two styles have one thing in common: they both originated in Spain and are heavily influenced by the sound of this country's music. But, in the modern era, both absorb influences from all over the world.

Most relevant for you in your practice, it is important to know that the two styles have a very different technical approach. Most flamenco guitarists would not be able to produce the sound that good classical guitarists can, and vice versa. Just as with the classical guitar, it takes a lot of work and dedication to develop skills to a high level in the flamenco style.

That said, a lot of the music in the classical guitar repertoire is *influenced* by flamenco. Because of this, it often benefits from a touch of rasgueado to add authenticity and to make reference to its cultural origin. Many older generation classical players used to avoid doing this, as it was often not considered a suitable expressive tool. However, in the modern day, many players tend to embrace it as a positive and appealing addition to their sound.

In order to get you on your way with this, I will have provided a few introductory exercises in the pages that follow. Remember, this is by no means a comprehensive guide to the flamenco genre or indeed the rasgueado technique. Instead, it is what you need to add a touch of Spanish authenticity to key passages within the innumerable pieces that are influenced by the Spanish and flamenco sound.

Keep in mind that, in flamenco music and rasgueado technique, there is a lot of idiosyncrasy amongst players and their preferred ways of strumming. You will find many people doing things differently to achieve a similar sound. The examples below are some of the most common approaches.

Practicing on muted strings

Whenever I practice rasgueado patterns, I like to dedicate some time to playing them with muted strings. I rest my fretting hand fingers gently across all the strings without pressing anything, dampening the sound of any pitch. Usually I do this around position five. Then I play the patterns I want to work on and concentrate fully on the sound of the picking hand fingers hitting the strings.

This is a very effective way to practice and monitor your progress. Additionally, once the patterns start to come together, you can hear a great example of the capability of the guitar to be a perfect and fascinating percussion instrument.

Key things to keep in mind when practicing rasgueado

- As with tremolo and other speed-orientated techniques, rasgueado becomes powerful when a consistent *evenness* is achieved between the notes in the patterns. If a rasgueado is uneven, it doesn't matter how fast you are playing, it will not sound as authentic or appealing

- Concentrate on the accurate movement of the fingers first and only speed up once precision is achieved. However, always aim for a *very quick* stroke, regardless of how slow the tempo is!

- Keep all fingers as relaxed as possible at all times

- The movement always originates from the knuckle of the hand, not the joints on the length of your fingers

- Repetition is critical. Without a great deal of this, coupled with patience, rasgueado is not achievable

Basic rasgueado pattern (four strokes)

Don't worry about ensuring that all the strings in the chord are stroked. Only aim to strum the top three or four.

Example 12a

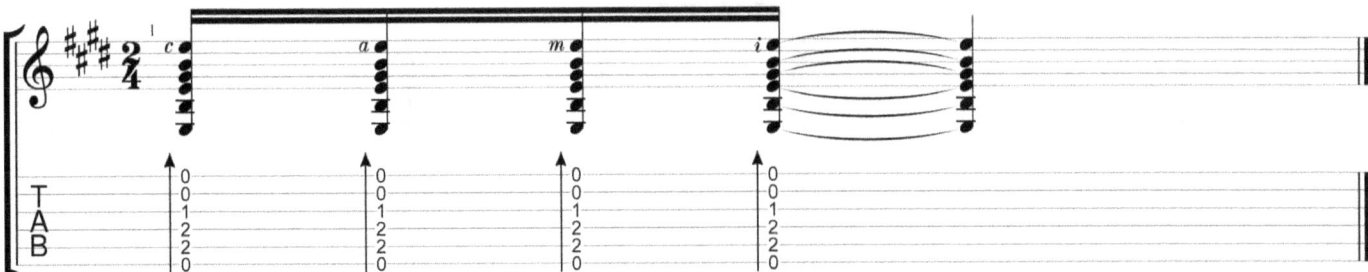

Here is an alternative way to play the same rhythm. Playing it in this way will produce a slightly different sound colour. When using this type of approach, it is key to ensure the first three strokes are played with only one downward movement of the hand. Do not stop your hand and bring it back to its starting position after playing any of the first three down strokes. One whole cycle of the pattern is executed with only one downward movement (first three strokes) and one upwards movement (last stroke) of the hand. This is vital, but very difficult to play fluidly at first, so be patient.

Example 12b

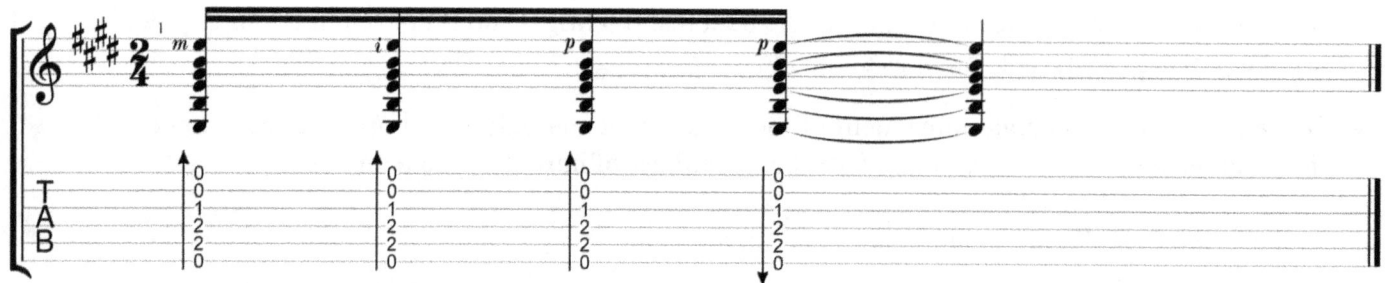

Basic rasgueado pattern (five strokes)

The fact that the final stroke here is an upstroke means that the chord is attacked from the upper register, making the stroke stand out. It should also be accented for added impact. Flamenco and rasgueado are all about confident, hard-hitting, stab-like statements with an emphasis on contrasting dynamics.

Example 12c

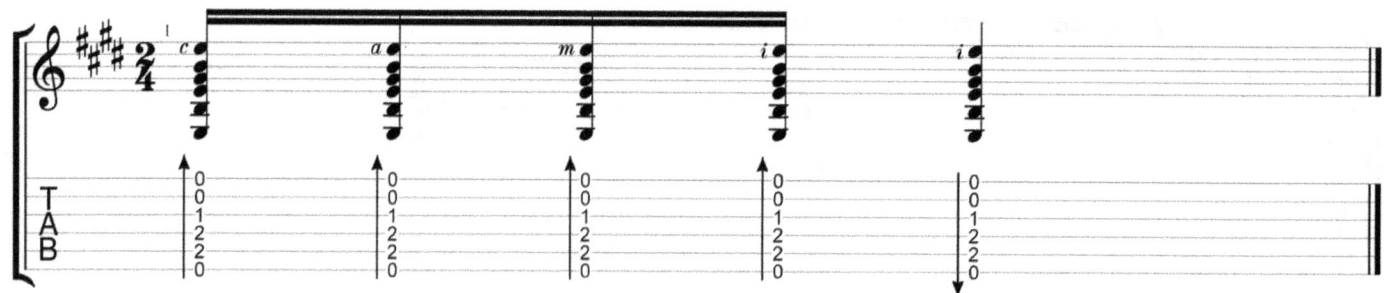

Here is an alternative way of playing the five-note rasgueado

Example 12d

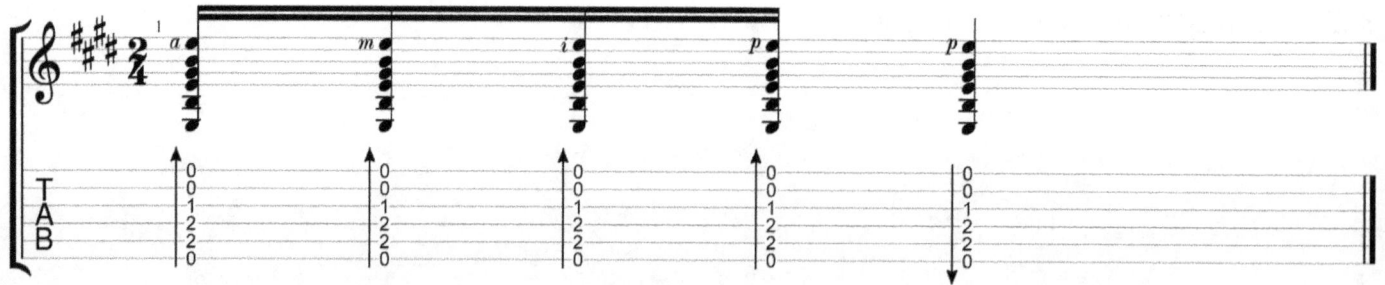

Below are some chord sequences for you to practice applying these principles. Through them, you can hear the impact these effects can have on a musical passage.

Example 12e

Example 12f

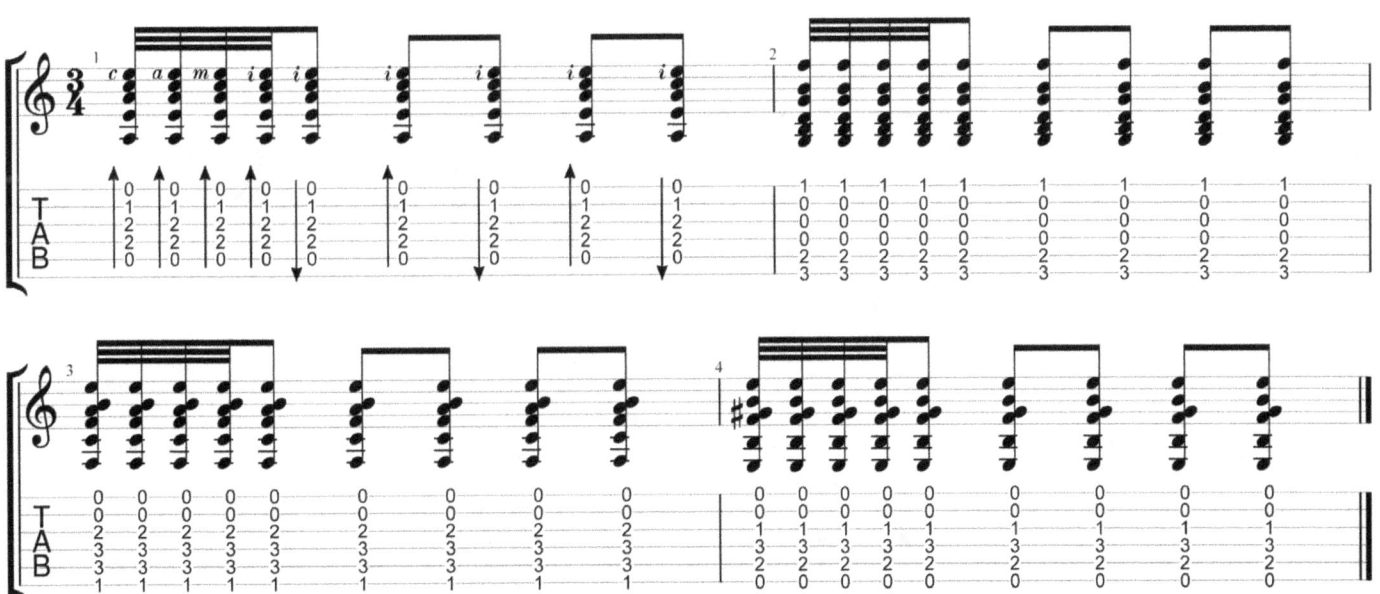

Example 12 g

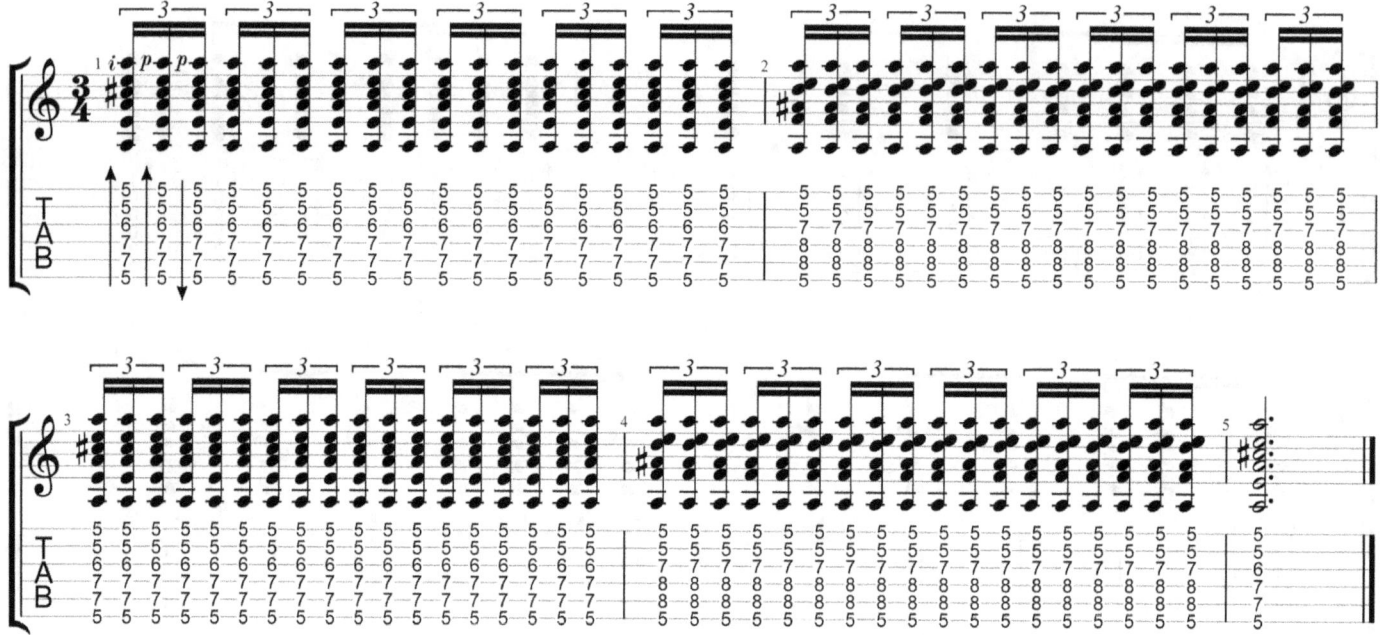

The same patterns can re-start with different fingers. This can be very challenging, and it also provides a slightly different sound colour.

Example 12h

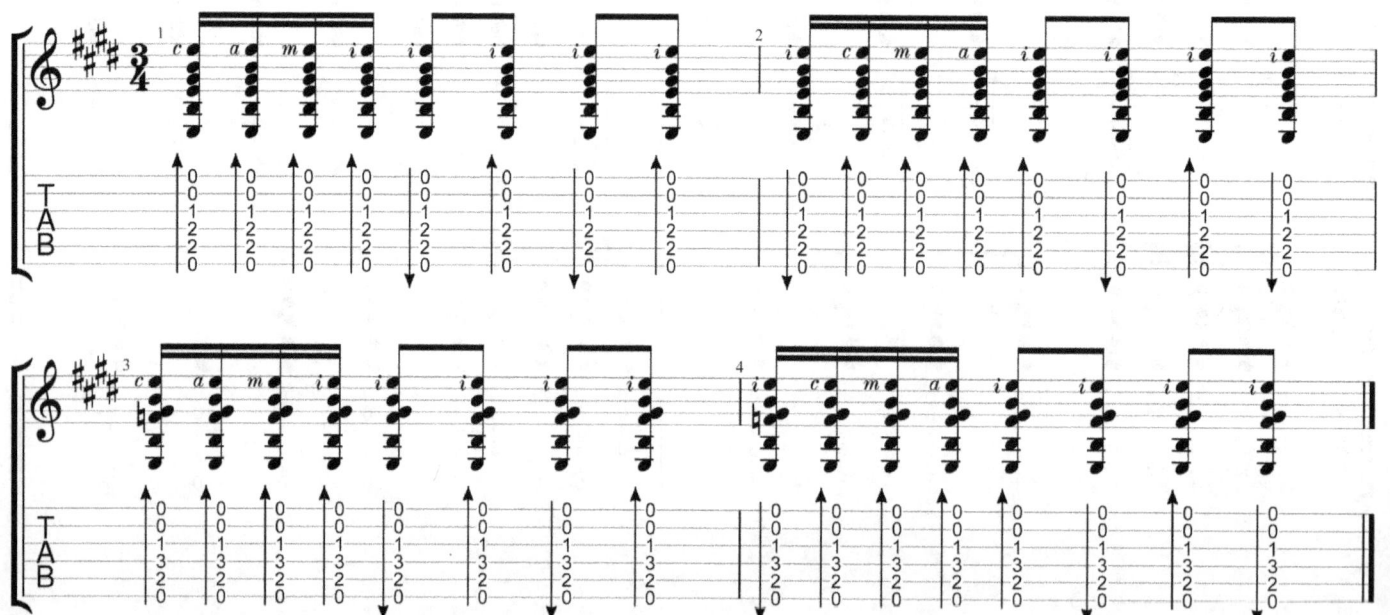

The guitar is a drum

The guitar is without doubt one of the most versatile instruments. One only has to look at the multiple contrasting styles of music in which it sits comfortably as a lead or accompanying voice to realise this. However, its rhythmic capabilities are particularly remarkable. A lot of what gives the guitar its charm is the element of percussion inevitably produced by the noise of the fingers hitting the strings, particularly when strumming chords.

Flamenco is a style that heavily relies on this aspect to produce its contagious sound. One intricate rasgueado pattern can command the attention more than the chord or chords being played. When you incorporate the techniques learnt in this chapter, keep this in mind. The rhythm has the lead role. The accuracy and *evenness* of the strumming is what will make it sound great.

Chapter Thirteen: Controlling Your Breathing

Basic considerations

There are so many things that a classical guitarist has to work on when taking their skill to a higher level that the issue of breathing is hardly ever mentioned. In reality, all parts of the body are involved in playing the instrument, and since they are interconnected their behaviour will affect all the other parts in one way or another.

In other spheres of life, the importance of controlling your breathing is spoken about. For example, when exercising or when trying to relax or keep calm. You have probably experienced your own breathing changing, depending on your mood or emotional state, without you necessarily controlling it. This is because the functions of our mind and body are connected and affect one another.

Unless we are in control, it is usually our emotional state that affects our breathing, rather than the other way around. Once we are aware of, and in control of our breathing, we can use it to improve our mental and emotional state, and also help our body to function better through stable oxygenation.

There are two factors that tend to affect the breathing most for guitarists:

- *Performance anxiety:* this is a deep subject and much research has been carried out on the topic. Most musicians, at times, experience some form of performance anxiety before playing in front of others. They may feel nervous because of the size of the audience, the significance of the gig for their reputation or career, because their colleagues or family are in the crowd, due to the type of audience, or for many other possible reasons
- *The challenges the piece presents:* naturally, big stretches, fast runs, leaping from one end of the fretboard to the other, a demanding picking hand pattern, or other similarly demanding technical features can have an effect on your mind. The feeling of "brace yourself!" when such a passage is looming can cause you to change your breathing and tense up your body in a way that can actually be very unhelpful

Challenges of breath control

It may seem simple at first but, particularly when you play anything demanding, controlling your breathing can be difficult. This is mostly because your mind is already occupied on the multiple tasks concerned with successfully playing the piece. If you haven't worked on this before, I recommend you try this experiment. Try playing something you find challenging and keep your breathing at a medium pace, steady and uninterrupted throughout. If the piece is reasonably long, this may be more difficult than you expect.

You may find that concentrating on your breathing takes a great deal of thinking at first, so that it forces you to lose focus on what is happening on the strings and so actually makes you sound worse! In this sense, controlling your breathing is no different to any good refinement of technique – it is all about replacing an old habit with a new one. It takes time to *force* yourself to approach things in a new way, before this new way becomes your *natural* way of doing things.

Controlling your breathing

A great way to practice steady, controlled breathing is to spend ten or so seconds establishing an ideal breathing rhythm before you start to play anything. Chose something simple and short to play. As you play, focus on your established breathing pattern and strive to maintain it, or at least keep it close to how it began, quickly controlling it every time it changes.

Repeat this every time you play and make it an essential part of your practice routine. As much as you can, actively incorporate it into your playing. Remember that if you only spend five minutes working on your breathing, then an hour or two not applying it, you are unlikely to master this long term.

Final Thoughts

Classical guitar playing is a fascinating, multifaceted endeavour. The priority is always the beauty of the sound. But this beauty is seldom achieved without a great deal of work on things that are not usually considered beautiful for the listener. This is certainly the case with some technical exercises which are more mechanical and seemingly more *athletic* than *musical*.

The sensation of looseness and control in the fingers that comes from developing good technique (and the feeling of ease it can generate when playing very demanding pieces) is undoubtedly a great one. Without it, some repertoire is impossible to play.

This book has been dedicated to this essential aspect of classical guitar. However, I urge you to remember that technique alone (even impeccable, astounding technique) will not make you a brilliant classical guitarist. You need to combine your developed technical prowess with a sense of communication and expression through your instrument in order to really make it *sing*. What does the music mean to the composer? What does the music mean to you? What kinds of thoughts or sensations does it cause in you?

Listen to some great players and pay close attention to the different ways in which they approach passages and pieces. They are all different in terms of their handling of dynamics, articulation, tempo choice, tempo variations, etc. The fact that the classical guitar is predominantly a solo instrument provides immense opportunities for the individual's own voice and identity to be truly represented in their playing.

More Classical Guitar Books From Fundamental Changes

First Pieces for Classical Guitar

Intermediate Pieces for Classical Guitar

The Beginner's Classical Guitar Method

Ten Classical Pieces for Guitar Ensemble

Discover more by scanning the QR code below with your smartphone: